CREATIVITY AND EDUCATION

CREATIVITY AND EDUCATION

HUGH LYTTON

Volume 46

Routledge
Taylor & Francis Group
LONDON AND NEW YORK

First published in 1971

This edition first published in 2012
by Routledge
2 Park Square, Milton Park, Abingdon, Oxfordshire OX14 4RN

Simultaneously published in the USA and Canada
by Routledge
711 Third Avenue, New York, NY 10017

First issued in paperback 2014

Routledge is an imprint of the Taylor and Francis Group, an informa company

British Library Cataloguing in Publication Data
A catalogue record for this book is available from the British Library

ISBN 13: 978-0-415-67549-9 (Volume 46)
ISBN 13: 978-0-415-75348-7 (pbk)

Publisher's Note
The publisher has gone to great lengths to ensure the quality of this reprint but
points out that some imperfections in the original copies may be apparent.

Disclaimer
The publisher has made every effort to trace copyright holders and would
welcome correspondence from those they have been unable to trace.

Creativity and Education

Hugh Lytton

LONDON

ROUTLEDGE & KEGAN PAUL

First published 1971
by Routledge & Kegan Paul Ltd
Broadway House, 68-74 Carter Lane,
London EC4V 5EL
Printed in Great Britain by
Northumberland Press, Ltd., Gateshead
ISBN 0 7100 7153 1 (c)
ISBN 0 7100 7154 X (p)

THE STUDENTS LIBRARY OF EDUCATION has been designed to meet the needs of students of Education at Colleges of Education and at University Institutes and Departments. It will also be valuable for practising teachers and educationists. The series takes full account of the latest developments in teacher-training and of new methods and approaches in education. Separate volumes will provide authoritative and up-to-date accounts of the topics within the major fields of sociology, philosophy and history of education, educational psychology, and method. Care has been taken that specialist topics are treated lucidly and usefully for the non-specialist reader. Altogether, the Students Library of Education will provide a comprehensive introduction and guide to anyone concerned with the study of education, and with educational theory and practice.

J. W. TIBBLE

The concept of creativity has now been a popular one in educational thought for about a decade. Originally work in this field was concerned mainly with identifying and attempting to measure 'creative abilities' and this gave a fresh impetus to a somewhat flagging mental test industry. But the work that has been done has a significance far beyond precarious attempts to identify, in early life, individuals who may make significant contributions to the sum of human achievements. It has served to focus attention on those powers of imagination and reason which all of us possess, in some measure, the cultivation of which is a perennial educational task.

The field of 'creativity' is a difficult and complex one, in which there has been much loose thinking and a good deal of trivial research. Mr Lytton has provided an excellent and clear guide for the beginning student, which allows him immediately to come to grips with the important aspects. Creativity is also an area in which value judgments have constantly to be made. The clarity and fairness with which the author has treated these complex issues add greatly to the value of the book for students.

BEN MORRIS

Contents

Acknowledgments

My first work in the area of creativity dates back to an abandoned Ph.D. thesis of many years ago. At the time Dr P. E. Vernon's critical interest in the subject spurred on mine and over the years since then I have received a great deal of stimulation and counsel from him for which I am very grateful. I wish to thank the Charles E. Merrill Publishing Company for permission to reprint a lesson segment from the article by R. M. Olton and R. S. Crutchfield in Covington *et al.*, *The Productive Thinking Program*. I should like to acknowledge also the contribution made by my wife through her critical comments on the draft of this book from which it has greatly benefited.

The limits of the possible constantly shift ... It is from the champions of the impossible rather than the slaves of the possible that evolution draws its creative force.

Barbara Wootton: *In a World I Never Made*

1

The creative process

'The Creator' *par excellence* is God and whenever we create some new thing we feel we are God-like and achieving immortality. The Greeks were aware of the awesomeness, the double-edged nature of creating, for Prometheus who discovered fire was venerated as a benefactor of mankind, raised to the Pantheon, but also, having aroused the envy of the Gods, punished cruelly for his pains. In its most basic sense (to 'pro-create') creating denotes sexuality—of beast as well as man—and hence is charged with all the emotion, the complexes and inhibitions, and the mysteries surrounding our deepest biological urges. Small wonder then that 'creativity' (a word of American coinage, not found in the *Oxford English Dictionary*) is a word of power, prestige and prodigiousness that we all wish to appropriate. Creativeness confers power and distinction. To quote Bruner (1962):

It is implied, I think, that the act of one creating is the act of a whole man, that it is this rather than the product that makes it good and worthy. So whoever seeks to proclaim his wholeness turns to the new slogan. There is creative advertising, creative engineering, creative problem-solving—all lively entries in the struggle for dignity in our time.

It seems best to start with a working definition of what we mean by a 'creative act'. Whilst later I shall examine in greater detail the nature and conditions of the creative act we can take as our starting point a simple, but all-embracing characteristic of the creative process that allows us to place it roughly in our universe, and no wording, I think, defines its most pervasive characteristic better than Bruner's 'effective surprise':

> What is curious about effective surprise is that it need not be rare or infrequent or bizarre and is often none of these things. Effective surprises ... seem rather to have the quality of obviousness to them when they occur, producing a shock of recognition, following which there is no longer astonishment. (Bruner, 1962)

There are two implications arising from this characterization of the creative act: firstly, creative quality can reside in any kind of human activity. Men can be creative not only in painting, writing poetry or discovering scientific theories, but also in cooking, carpentering, playing football or making love. Secondly, it is not only the genius who produces creative acts, but this quality can be present in many minor acts at many different levels of ability or intelligence. We should here recognize a distinction between an objectively and a subjectively creative act. The product of *objective* creativity must meet certain criteria so that 'effective surprise' is felt by the beholder. The first and most important is perhaps appropriateness: the product must make sense in the light of the demands of the situation and the specifications of the producer. It should call forth satisfaction, because it fits its context—it is not only right, but *just* right. (This is another way of expressing 'effective surprise'.) The second criterion is novelty: the product should be unusual as judged by appropriate norms, or should lead to an uncommon way of experiencing the world. Thirdly—and this is the highest standard—we may judge a creative product by its power to transform the traditional constraints of reality and to yield a radically new perspective. Some original thoughts bring about a radical shift in our approach to a whole field of knowledge. (Cf. Jackson and Messick, 1968, for a detailed discussion of these points.)

Subjective creativity is judged by different canons: it can occur when a person combines things in ways that are individual to him, when he does not simply imitate, but regroups given stimuli or data by means of his own thoughts or actions, irrespective of the effect his creation has on others. We cannot, for instance, deny the epithet 'creative' to the five year-old who with all his might and enthusiasm has given us an image of the world as *he* sees it, littered with square cows and peopled with round-bellied, neckless mums and dads. When he has, out of his own powers, made this vision of the world his own he has been—subjectively—creative, even if thousands of others have acted similarly.

A well-known story tells how a class was given the problem of adding the series: $1+2+3+4+5+6+7+8+9+10$. Everybody was working away, laboriously adding the ten separate figures, but one six-year-old boy, after only a few seconds' thought, announced the answer, 55, to the astonished teacher. He had discovered that there was a logical structure to the series, which could be looked on as consisting of five pairs of numbers, 1 and 10, 2 and 9 etc., each adding up to 11. This boy, who was to be the mathematician Gauss, had by himself discovered a property of a series and thus shown considerable creativeness, as far as his subjective mental processes were concerned, even though the rule was known to most adults before him.

If we call 'effective surprise' the hallmark of the creative act, we are in effect setting up a psychological state as the criterion of creativity. And indeed creative acts, or at least the finishing of them, are always marked by states of

3

relief, exhilaration, thrill for the creator so that the act makes a psychological impact on the doer and, in most cases, also on the beholder. While this is a corollary of creativity, it is, of course, not a distinguishing mark exclusive to it.

Imagination and intuition

Before we look at the creative process more closely we must discuss some other concepts that are often mentioned in connection with it: *imagination* and *intuition*. Imagination has a number of different meanings. Thus, we can say 'I can imagine what this house will look like, when it is finished' or 'Imagine the Roman soldiers standing guard on Hadrian's wall!', and in these cases by imagining we mean calling up before the mind's eye images of things that are not actually present, that are to be in the future or that existed in the distant past. This meaning is codified by the dictionary as 'Power of forming mental concepts or images of things not experienced'. We do, of course, conjure up before the mind's eye not only possible things, but also things or events that are completely divorced from reality, that are simply 'figments of our imagination'. In the midst of winter, sitting shivering in front of a small fire, we might for instance imagine ourselves being wafted away to a fairy island of permanent warmth and sunshine where manna rained from the heavens to give us sustenance. When we evoke images of this kind we are using our imagination in a day-dream. From this day-dream, and from deliberate pretence and make-believe, it is but a small step to hallucinations or actual dreams, where we say that our 'imagination' gets the better of us.

Another use of the term is apparent when we talk of people 'thinking imaginatively', or of younger children 'playing imaginatively', or when we say that an account

has been written 'with imagination'. Here we attach a positive value judgment to the term, meaning by it that the thing
has been done inventively (though we do not approve of
too much invention, since we use 'his imagination has run
away with him' as a polite euphemism for a whopping lie).
This use corresponds to another dictionary definition of
'imagination', namely 'artistically inventive or creative
faculty' and here, quite clearly, creativity is implied.

'Imagination', indeed, always implies going beyond the
given data. Thus, for instance, in young Gauss's problem,
simply adding up to find the answer was not imaginative,
but going beyond the immediately obvious facts and seeing
the hidden structure *was* an act of imagination and, thereby, of creativeness. (Bruner (1962) suggests the term 'formal
effectiveness' for the kind of thing that young Gauss did:
'It consists of an ordering of elements in such a way that
one sees relationships that were not evident before, group-
ings that were not present.') Although we are able to
imagine things that are unreal, that we have never seen
and that are inherently impossible, these things are in fact
always somehow tied to a part of our reality. It is notable,
for instance, that in medieval pictures painted by German
artists, scenes from the Holy Land show a remarkable
resemblance to medieval German towns with their half-
timbered, gabled houses.

At first blush it would appear easy to contrast logical,
systematic thinking with imaginative thinking. A Harvard
publication, for instance, states: 'Logical thinking is
straight, as opposed to crooked thinking, and that of the
poet may be described as curved thinking' (Conant, 1945).
Hutchinson (1949) differentiates between systematic
thinking and insight. In systematic thinking, the objective,
problem, and method are clearly defined, the process is
deliberate, methodical, the problem is well within the
range of abilities of the thinker. Awareness of logical relations and the application of the laws of associative think-

5

ing are emphasized. Such systematic thinking applies in situations where plans can be deliberately formulated, where the number of variables and hypotheses is not too large. Insight, on the other hand, according to Hutchinson, occurs in the solution of baffling problems and is accompanied by the emergence of the unexpected by feelings first of frustration, and then of apparently effortless integration, feelings of exhilaration, finality and accomplishment.

Hutchinson considers these two types to be the extremes on a scale of thinking and similarly Bartlett (1958) postulates a range of kinds of thinking, the extremes of which he calls 'thinking within closed systems' and 'adventurous thinking'. Now it is tempting, but would be very inaccurate, to identify imaginative or insightful thinking with 'adventurous thinking' and systematic thinking, lacking the imaginative touch, with 'thinking in closed systems'. Bartlett (1958) defines a 'closed system' as 'one possessing a limited number of units, or items, or members, and those properties of the members which are to be used are known to begin with and do not change as the thinking proceeds'. An example of an easy task within a closed system would be the well-known Verbal Reasoning Test question, requiring interpolation of figures in a series, e.g.:

$$1\ 2\ 4\ 7\ \ldots\ 22\ 29$$

Extrapolation, too, where the direction which thinking is to take is predetermined, but the terminal point is not given, is of the 'closed-system' variety. Indeed, the difference between extrapolation and interpolation seems to consist mainly in the formal presentation of the given data, e.g. the above problem would not change in nature if it was given as:

$$1\ 2\ 4\ 7\ 11\ 16\ \ldots$$

The characteristic of the 'closed system' is the presence of a structure of logical constraints which determine a limited number of possible solutions, but these solutions need not be either easy or obvious. Where the evidence that has to be used in arriving at a solution is disguised, the problem-solving process may, in fact, be very complex. Bartlett gives as example an addition sum:

D O N A L D
G E R A L D
———————————
R O B E R T

The data provided are: (1) D$=5$; (2) every number from 0–9 has its corresponding letter; (3) no two letters have the same numerical value. (The reader may wish to discover the elements of this 'closed system' for himself.) Another example of difficult thinking within a closed system would be the detective work of a Maigret who has to fill in the gaps in very incomplete evidence, though when all the data *are* available only one answer is possible.

When the conditions of a given problem have been closely specified the solution can be arrived at by one small step or by means of a step-by-step trial of a limited number of alternatives to determine which one will fit the specifications. A computer can easily be programmed to carry out this task. The sparser the data provided, the larger the gaps in the evidence to be bridged, the greater is the number of alternative steps that might be tried. The practically limitless welter of permutations of moves possible, for instance, in a chess-game will, however, be reduced to a more manageable choice by the 'intuitive familiarity' of the good player with the strategies and possibilities of the game. Even within a closed system, then, in order to select the *right* combinations leading to effective solutions, a person needs to be attuned to the problem, to be sensitive to likely leads and have a sense of which facts or combinations are relevant (this is probably what is meant by *intuition* in a certain field—the process of attaining solutions without knowledge of all the relevant data,

7

without going through a process of step-by-step logical reasoning). In other words, where steps are not closely specified, where gaps are large or many and links remote (which means most problems outside textbooks) an imaginative leap beyond the data is necessary as part of 'closed-system' thinking, if this is to be effective. On the other hand, where gaps are small or links obvious, thinking can be stepwise. Such steps for the mental mountaineer are, unfortunately, not normally provided in nature, but have to be hewn out of the rock of data by some pioneer thinker. In working out such steps—an essentially imaginative task —the pioneer will routinize and thereby facilitate subsequent effective thinking either for himself or for other, more routine workers. In a significant aside Herman Bondi, the well-known physicist, once said: 'Mathematicians are not specially good at thinking, they are good at inventing ways to avoid thinking.' The programmer will perform the same task for his computer by programming it with the necessary sequence of steps or strategies of search likely to lead to success and will thus routinize and give direction to a search that may require a very large number of steps and combinations of steps. By having 'intuitive familiarity' with a certain problem area built into it, the computer is in this way enabled to simulate the competent scientist or good chess-player (see above and cf. Newell, Shaw and Simon, 1962). It should be said, however, that so far, no chess-playing programme has ever been achieved that has been thought a worthy opponent by any, even moderate, human chess-player.

On closer analysis, then, we find that imaginative thinking is, indeed, often an important part of 'closed-system thinking' and the most crucial difference between systematic and imaginative thinking turns out to be one of size of step, though there may also be other differences, such as the level of consciousness at which the attempts at a solution occur. (The verification of a solution and its checking against criteria would, of course, again necessitate systematic thinking.)

Another way of looking at the distinction is to think of routine, systematic thinking as characterized by responses that are high in the stimulus-response hierarchy. A response that is strong or high in the hierarchy is more likely to occur in the presence of a stimulus, i.e. it is a common response. Original thinking, on the other hand, is typified by responses that are weak or low in the hierarchy, in other words, uncommon responses. Problem solving in this view (cf. Maltzman, 1955) involves the selection of responses, often weak ones, as well as of whole 'habit-family hierarchies'. However, this view fails to convey any sense of directiveness in the process of imaginative thinking.

At the opposite end of the scale to 'closed-system thinking' Bartlett (1958) places 'adventurous thinking' and he finds this exemplified in experimental thinking, in everyday thinking and in the artist's thinking. He contrasts the two as follows:

> The thinker in the closed system is in the position of contemplating a finished structure. Very often this may be exceedingly complex and elaborate and the rules of its constitution difficult to appreciate. The thinker is, however, in the position of a spectator searching for something which he must treat as being in some way 'there' all the time.... The experimental thinker is in the position of somebody who must use whatever tools may be available for adding to some structure that is not yet finished, and that he himself is certainly not going to complete.

In 'experimental' or 'adventurous' thinking the gaps have become wider and the situation more loosely structured. The first main task has shifted from solving problems to formulating the problem in the most effective way, or to asking the right questions. Whilst there is more need and scope for imagination in 'adventurous thinking' than in the 'closed-system' variety, clearly, imaginative thinking is not co-extensive with or confined to thinking in unstructured situations, but can occur in many different fields and contexts.

Creative moments

But let us return to the creative process itself—and, as we have noted, imagination in one of its senses ('inventive or creative faculty') is synonymous with it. At the heart of creativity lie the creative moment and the creative impulse, the most intensely personal experiences an individual is capable of. It is here that the 'I' experiences—for creating means perceiving as well as doing—and acts following out its own most idiosyncratic ways. By definition, it is producing a novel recombination which is not predictable from general laws. No scientific, testable theory has, as yet, come to grips with this phenomenon and the best approach available to us is still through descriptive, literary accounts.

After forty-odd years the analysis of the creative process that is most widely quoted is still that by Graham Wallas (1926) and it must, therefore, be assumed to have a certain intuitive plausibility and appeal to a large number of artists and psychological writers. Wallas is concerned mainly with novel thought in the mathematical and scientific area, but it can be seen that his ideas have application in other fields too. He suggests the process can be divided into four stages: 1. Preparation—the stage in which the problem is investigated from all directions and this 'includes the whole process of intellectual education' with its training in experimental and logical procedures, as well as the process of acquainting oneself with background facts and knowledge. 2. Incubation—this is the stage during which the individual is not consciously thinking about the problem, when it is simmering in him, although he may seek relaxation from conscious effort (examples will follow later). 3. Illumination—this stage is not confined to the 'flash of insight', but includes the psychological events that immediately precede and accompany its appearance. 4. Verification—the stage in which the validity of the concepts is tested and the ideas reduced to exact form.

This division can be criticized—on the grounds, for instance, that although no doubt all four are involved in the delivery of the finished product, only incubation and illumination, and possibly to some extent preparation, throw light on the creative process itself. The different stages are, in other words, of varying importance. A more fundamental criticism is the point made by Vinacke (1952) who concluded on the basis of reports by various creative writers and scientists that 'it is necessary to conceive of creative thinking in terms of dynamic, interplaying activities, rather than as more or less discrete stages'. However, this kind of critique can always be applied to any more or less artificial analysis into stages—the stages are, after all, superimposed on an ongoing activity and the author would probably quite readily admit that in any given case the simultaneity of the processes is quite as striking as their discreteness.

The beginning of creation is marked, as many writers confirm, by a hunch, diffuse excitement, the awareness of some ill-defined, half-conscious problem—and this may, indeed, precede the stage of 'preparation', of gathering the material. Stephen Spender writes of 'a dim cloud of an idea which I feel must be condensed into a shower of words' and Alfred North Whitehead of 'the state of imaginative muddled suspense which precedes successful inductive generalizations'.

The need for a period of 'incubation' or gestation when ideas sink down to subconscious levels where all kinds of mental processes can get to work at them is almost universally recognized. William Blake is one of the few who does not acknowledge this stage in himself, since he claimed that some of his poetry came without any apparent pre-meditation, as if dictated to him. On the other hand, Bertrand Russell has remarked on the fruitless effort he used to expend in trying to push his creative work to completion by force of will before he recognized how much easier it was to await the result of the more organic process of subconscious maturing. Poincaré (1913), too, writes: 'Most striking at first is this appearance of sudden illumination, a manifest sign of long, unconscious prior work.'

It should not be thought, however, that the individual must be completely *un*conscious, in the literal sense of the word, of the processes at work within him. Consciousness is a matter of degree and there are intermediate 'regions' (speaking in topographical metaphors) between full 'focal awareness', as Koestler (1964) calls it, and the unconscious 'regions'. The intermediate areas have been called 'the pre-conscious' or, stemming from the analogy of vision, 'peripheral awareness' and Wallas (1926) writes of the moment 'when our fringe-consciousness of an association-train is in the state of rising consciousness which indicates that the fully conscious flash of success is coming'. The problem which 'bothers' the individual, with which he is preoccupied, will very often be present just outside the bright spot illuminated by the light of his fully directed awareness, and indeed the focus of awareness will often shift, so that at one moment it will direct its full glare on the problem and at others will leave it in the semi-dark or pitch dark outer regions.

The state of mind which has typically been thought propitious to creative work is the day-dream. For Freud, certainly in his early writings, creative work, in common with the day-dreams and play, arises from wishes that, because they violate society's prohibitions, have been repressed and seek their fulfilment in fantasy. Creative production is therefore a form of 'substitute gratification' and an extension of the child's play and the ordinary man's day-dream. Freud displays an ambivalent attitude to the artist. While he exposes the lowly origins of his inspiration, he allows himself at the same time an expression of unease about this implicit devaluation of the artist's standing:

> We are perfectly aware that very many imaginative writings are far removed from the model of the naïve day-dream; and yet I cannot suppress the suspicion that even the most extreme deviations from that model could be linked with it through an uninterrupted series of transitional cases. (Freud, 1908)

Most other writers on the psychology of creation, including psycho-analytic writers, however, take a more positive view of the value of relaxation of conscious controls. Koestler, whose views will be more fully discussed below, for instance, writes (Koestler, 1964):

> The temporary relinquishing of conscious controls liberated the mind from certain constraints which are necessary to maintain the disciplined routines of thoughts but may become an impediment to the creative leap; at the same time other types of ideation on more primitive levels of mental organization are brought into activity.

A celebrated example of the benefits of a temporary abandonment of the discipline of consciousness is the following report by Kekulé, a professor of chemistry at Ghent who describes an experience he had in 1865:

> I turned my chair to the fire and dozed [he relates]. Again the atoms were gambolling before my eyes. This time the smaller groups kept modestly in the background. My mental eye, rendered more acute by repeated visions of this kind, could now distinguish larger structures, of manifold conformation; long rows, sometimes more closely fitted together; all twining, and twisting, in a snakelike motion. But look! What was that? One of

the snakes had seized hold of its own tail, and the form whirled mockingly before my eyes. As if by a flash of lightning I awoke ... Let us learn to dream, gentlemen. (Quoted in Koestler, 1964)

The snake biting its own tail conjured up before Kekulé's dreaming eye the visual image, the model, which helped him to see the molecules of certain organic compounds as closed rings instead of as open structures.

But how, from amongst the multifarious elements of the semi-conscious day-dream or unconscious thought, are those images or ideas selected that will bear fruit in a new theory, experiment or work of art? How, in fact, is the day-dream translated into creative work? Poincaré, who was a mathematician, writes: 'To create (in mathematics) consists precisely in not making useless combinations and in making those which are useful and which are only a small minority. Invention is discernment, choice', and goes on to propose that in this selection aesthetic sensitivity plays a decisive role: 'The privileged unconscious phenomena, those susceptible of becoming conscious, are those which, directly or indirectly, affect most profoundly our emotional sensibility' (Poincaré, 1913). However detailed knowledge of the appropriate field is by no means irrelevant. To quote Bruner (1962): 'In each empirical field there is developed in the creating scientist a kind of "intuitive familiarity", to use a term that L. J. Henderson was fond of, that gives him a sense of which combinations are likely to have predictive effectiveness and which are absurd.' Pasteur epitomized it in the self-congratulatory phrase: 'Fortune favours the prepared mind.'

It is worth considering one of the few coherent theories of the nature of creativity available—the one evolved by Koestler and expressed most fully in *The Act of Creation* (1964). Koestler, whose conceptions owe a great deal to the school of psycho-analytic thought, places creativity in the context of the processes of life in general which follow certain rules designed to lend the organism coherence, stability, as well as some flexibility.

One of the recurring life processes is that of regeneration, when mutilated lower organisms, such as the flatworm, retrace the steps of their original development, as it were, and are thereby enabled to create themselves anew from small fragments. Examples of less radical reconstitution of parts of the body exist also in higher animals. Koestler detects a similar pattern in the creative act: *'reculer pour mieux sauter'*. In the creative act the mind 'regresses', i.e. gives itself up to the 'games of the underground', the inventive name that Koestler gives to the subconscious mental processes. In these 'games' the mind combines apparently incompatible ideas, turns up hidden analogies between cabbages and kings and once again possesses the fluidity of the primitive consciousness of the child for whom the world and 'I' are one.

Such mental states are common to the child, the psychotic, the dreamer and the creative mind. But, writes Koestler (1964): 'In pathological states the games of the underground play havoc with the disciplined routines of thought —a *reculer sans sauter*. But on rare, privileged occasions they have the effect of liberating the mind from its straitjacket and releasing its creative potentials.' Kekulé's dream, quoted above, is one of many possible examples.

In this way hitherto unrelated frames of reference may be associated and objects and ideas seen in a new light. In an earlier work (1959) Koestler expressed it thus:

This act of wrenching away an object or concept from its habitual associative context and seeing it in a new context is, as I have tried to show, an essential part of the creative process. It is an act both of destruction and of creation, for it demands the breaking up of a mental habit, the melting down, with the blowlamp of Cartesian doubt, of the frozen structure of accepted theory, to enable the new fusion to take place ... Every creative act—in science, art, or religion—involves a regression to a more primitive level, a new innocence of perception liberated from the cataract of accepted beliefs. It is a process of *reculer pour mieux sauter*, of disintegration preceding the new synthesis, comparable to the dark night of the soul through which the mystic must pass.

In the later book Koestler coined the term 'act of bisociation' for what to him is the essence of creation, namely the bringing together of two unconnected matrices of thought. (A 'matrix' is Koestler's formula for a bodily function, perceptual skill or mental habit, or a system of these.) This 'bisociative act' is, in fact, characteristic of creation in any sphere of human activity.

Thus poetry conveys not only meaning, but the patterns of the sounds evoke primitive echoes in us, and it is the two frames of reference of meaning and sound which interact. Koestler sees a similar bisociation of matrices in all other arts and all forms of art, Koestler suggests, serve man's 'self-transcending' emotions or participatory tendencies, i.e. the emotion in which the individual feels himself to be part of some larger whole. This can be aroused by listening to Mozart, seeing the Mona Lisa or kneeling in prayer.

The complementary emotions in Koestler's system are the self-assertive emotions through which a person's individual functions are affirmed. These find their expression in humour, the essence of which is the clash of two incompatible frames of reference. (Koestler provides a fund of entertaining examples.)

Scientific discovery is associated with neither of these two kinds of emotion. It is not neutral or bereft of all feelings, but Koestler thinks of it as a well-balanced compound of passions into which both self-asserting and participatory tendencies enter in highly sublimated form. In Koestler's neat philosophical-psychological system, to the different forms of creation, accompanied by their varying emotions, there correspond also differing ways of joining hitherto separate universes of discourse: 'The result is either a *collision* of matrices ending in laughter; or their fusion in a synthesis providing new insights; or their *juxta-position* in the raptness of aesthetic experience' (Koestler, 1964).

Koestler's theory has not remained without its critics, par-ticularly from the scientific and psychological confrèrie, and it must be said there is substance to some of the criticism. Koestler seems to place the criterion of dif-ference between a scientific theory and a work of art in the emotional state of their creators; whereas the dis-tinguishing mark of a scientific theory is usually held to be that it will lead to predictions which may, by experi-mental observations, be tested, so that, in principle, the theory can be disproved. Koestler, essentially, leaves the act of verification out of account in order to concentrate on the moment of inspiration. His 'cosmology of the soul' is altogether too neat, systematic and all-embracing and it is difficult to see how it could be disproved by any experi-ment. In sum, it is a literary, not a scientific theory, a con-tribution to philosophical psychology.

But, this criticism aside, his account of the creative forces is a plausible one and supported by evidence from the self-observations of many creative individuals. The idea of the mind reverting to more primitive levels of operation in order to accomplish the fusion of the creative act derives from the concept of 'regression in the service of the ego', developed by the psycho-analytic writer Kris, and has been widely accepted. It is, at least, not incompatible with the little experimental evidence we possess (cf. Wild, 1965). Koestler's theory is a semantic interpretation and con-ceptualization of experimental data and it will always be possible to generate several alternative interpretations. In the absence of a more truly scientific theory of creativity, however (if such a one should be possible), we can regard his theory of the creative act—though not of the nature of science—as a facet of the truth and can admire its creative elegance.

The poet's inspiration

What do poets themselves have to say about the moments of inspiration and about their methods of work?

Stephen Spender (1946) writes: 'Inspiration is the beginning of a poem and it is also its final goal. It is the first idea which drops into the poet's mind and it is the final idea which he at last achieves in words. In between this start and this winning post there is the hard race, the sweat and toil.' He tells us of a phrase, 'the language of flesh and roses', that once flashed into his mind and that may in years to come be the nucleus of a future poem, and he adds: 'My own experience of inspiration is certainly that of a line or a phrase or a word or sometimes something still vague, a dim cloud of an idea which I feel must be condensed into a shower of words.'

The most famous account of writing that dispenses with the 'sweat and toil' is contained in Coleridge's Preface to *Kubla Khan*:

> In the summer of the year 1797, the Author, then in ill-health, had retired to a lonely farm-house between Porlock and Linton ... In consequence of a slight indisposition, an anodyne had been prescribed (elsewhere Coleridge called it 'two grains of Opium'!) from the effects of which he fell asleep in his chair at the moment that he was reading the following sentence, or words of the same substance, in 'Purchas's Pilgrimage': 'Here the Khan Kubla commanded a palace to be built, and a stately garden thereunto. And thus ten miles of fertile ground were inclosed with a wall.' The Author continued for about three hours in a profound sleep, at least of the external sense, during which time he has the most vivid confidence, that he could not have composed less than

from two to three hundred lines; if that indeed can be called composition in which all the images rose up before him as things, with a parallel production of the correspondent expressions, without any sensation or consciousness of effort. On awaking he appeared to himself to have a distinct recollection of the whole, and taking his pen, ink, and paper, instantly and eagerly wrote down the lines that are here preserved. At this moment he was unfortunately called out by a person on business from Porlock, and detained by him above an hour, and on his return to his room, found, to his no small surprise and mortification, that though he still retained some vague and dim recollection of the general purport of the vision, yet, with the exception of some eight or ten scattered lines and images, all the rest had passed away ... (Coleridge, 1954)

Jean Cocteau stresses the nature of the unconscious work in the artist and the overpowering force with which it demands to find expression:

These unknown forces work deep within us, with the aid of the elements of daily life, ... and, when they burden us and oblige us to conquer the kind of somnolence in which we indulge ourselves like invalids who try to prolong dream and dread resuming contact with reality, in short when the work that makes itself in us and in spite of us demands to be born, we can believe that this work comes to us from beyond and is offered us by the gods. (Cocteau, 1952)

But among modern poets the one who perhaps most strongly felt the primitive force of his inspiration that came, as it willed, and would not be commanded, was the German poet, Rainer Maria Rilke. He began the poems, that later came to be known as the 'Duino Elegies', with a line that came to him, seemingly out of a storm, as he paced to and fro outside his residence in the winter of 1912. For many years he struggled with the elegies, writing now one, now part of another, endeavouring to create in them a vision of the world, not as humans see it, but 'as it is within the angel'. But it was not until 1922 that the labour was completed and he announced the end triumphantly in a letter to Princess Marie von Thurn und Taxis-Hohenlohe, the owner of Duino Castle where the elegies had their origin:

> At last, Princess, at last, the blessed, how blessed day, on which I can announce to you the conclusion—so far as I see—of the Elegies:
> *ten!*
> From the last, the great one (with the opening, begun long since in Duino: 'Some day, emerging at last from this terrifying vision, may I burst into jubilant praise to assenting angels ...') from this last one, which moreover, even then, was intended to be the last,—from this —my hand is still trembling! Just now, Saturday, the eleventh, at six o'clock in the evening, it's finished!—
> All in a few days, there was a nameless storm, a hurricane, in my mind (like that time in Duino), everything in the way of fibre and web in me split,—eating was not to be thought of, God knows who fed me.
> But now *it is*. IS,
> Amen.
> So I've survived up to this, through and through it all. Through it all. And it was this that was needed. *Only* this.

(Rilke, 1939, Introduction by J. B. Leishman)

Here we have the emotional charge, the passion, of the creative moment. But there are also trivial conditions that may be necessary to it. Pure inspiration may come anywhere, but for the elaboration of this vision, for the hard work that makes the vision tangible and turns it into a work of art the poet or writer needs conditions that he finds conducive to concentration. Rilke, for instance, needed the quiet and isolation of country mansions. Other writers required various more mundane paraphernalia to jog along the tired muse. Schiller was aided by the smell of rotten apples hidden in his desk and by a liberal supply of coffee. Balzac needed coffee and wet towels round his head to help him write in the middle of the night. Dr Johnson was said to work best with a purring cat and some orange peel near by and plenty of tea to drink. The requirements are as multifarious, odd and unpredictable as the writers.

The scientist's insight

Scientists, too, have vouchsafed us glimpses into the processes that lead them to a complete restructuring of their 'matrices' of thought, to creative ideas in their own fields. Kekulé's dream has already been quoted (p. 13). Such sudden illuminations usually seem to emerge after the scientist has already spent weeks living with the problem, 'worrying' about it on and off—the period of 'incubation'. Thus the mathematician Jacques Hadamard records:

> On being very abruptly awakened by an external noise, a solution long searched for appeared to me at once without the slightest instant of reflection on my part—the fact was remarkable enough to have struck me unforgettably—and in a quite different direction from any of those which I had previously tried to follow. (Hadamard, 1952)

Poincaré gives us a vivid report of how he struggled with the problem of the 'Fuchsian functions':

> Every day I seated myself at my work table, stayed an hour or two, tried a great number of combinations and reached no results. One evening, contrary to my custom, I drank black coffee and could not sleep. Ideas rose in crowds; I felt them collide until pairs interlocked, so to speak, making a stable combination. By the next morning I had established the existence of a class of Fuchsian functions, those which come from the hypergeometric series; I had only to write out the results, which took but a few hours.

Then comes the famous description of the inspiration on the bus:

> Just at this time I left Caen, where I was then living, to go on a geologic excursion under the auspices of the School of Mines. The changes of travel made me forget my mathematical work. Having reached Coutances, we entered an omnibus to go some place or other. At the moment when I put my foot on the step the idea came to me, without anything in my former thoughts seeming to have paved the way for it, that the transformations I had used to define the Fuchsian functions were identical with those of non-Euclidean geometry. I did not verify the idea; I should not have had time, as, upon taking my seat in the omnibus, I went on with a conversation already commenced, but I felt a perfect certainty. (Poincaré, 1913)

In the arts the creative process itself is a long drawn-out affair. The execution of the original idea, the flash of illumination, requires further long-term creative efforts of a high order, because the detailed expression is an essential and difficult part of the creative endeavour. In science, on the other hand, what follows the moment of insight seems a very pedestrian process, a matter of verification and formulation and this may be a long, tedious slog or a quick routine job. For Einstein, for instance, the 'axioms' in which his relativity theory was expressed were only a matter of later formulation, after the real thing, the main discovery, had occurred.

> This was merely a later formulation of the subject matter, just a question of how the thing could afterwards best be written. The axioms express essentials in a condensed form. Once one has found such things one enjoys formulating them in that way; but in this process they did not grow out of any manipulation of axioms. (Wertheimer, 1961)

It would almost seem that the equivalent of the scientist's

checking would be the writer's proof-reading or establishment of a book's index.

A particularly fascinating picture of science in the making has been drawn by James Watson (1968), permitting us a revealing insight into how revolutionary discoveries arise out of a mixture of immersion in a field, patience, dogged persistence, collaboration, competitive spirit, moments of lucid insight and, above all, pure luck. Watson describes how he, Francis Crick and Maurice Wilkins teased out the structure of DNA, a discovery which earned them the Nobel prize. They had arrived at the knowledge that their problem lay in the sequence of the chemical bases, the 'polynucleotide backbone' of the molecules of DNA and they worked on physical models of these in their lab. In between Watson went off to spend the afternoons playing tennis or to watch X category films. But, he reports: 'Even during good films I found it almost impossible to forget the bases. The fact that we had at last produced a stereochemically reasonable configuration for the backbone was always in the back of my head.' He and Francis Crick were spurred on in their efforts by the knowledge of the importance of the discovery, if they could only reach it, and by the desire to beat Linus Pauling, an eminent American chemist, to the award of the Nobel prize. A little later a possible solution occurred to Watson which postulated that the DNA molecule consisted of two chains with identical base sequences so that adenine on one chain was linked to adenine on the other, guanine to guanine, etc., by means of hydrogen bonds. The idea sent his pulse racing—he thought he had found the solution. But a collaborator in the lab soon disabused him: 'My scheme was torn to shreds by the following noon. Against me was the awkward chemical fact that I had chosen the wrong tautomeric forms of guanine and thymine.'

After this disappointment the men continued playing about with the models as well as following other more light-hearted pursuits. Then, one day: 'I began shifting the bases in and out of various other pairing possibilities. Suddenly I became aware that an adenine-thymine pair held together by two hydrogen bonds was identical in shape to a guanine-cytosine pair held together by at least two hydrogen bonds.'

An almost accidental finding, but this time it was 'it'. The essential, fruitful illumination had come, the 'fusion of matrices' had occurred. It remained for them to check this arrangement of a 'double helix' against the known chemical facts, to make sure that all the stereochemical contacts were satisfactory and that the postulated structure accorded with the calculations based on X-ray data. When all this checking had been done they knew they were home and felt confident enough to send off their paper to *Nature*. A scientific discovery was complete.

2

'Convergent' and 'divergent' thinking, or how intelligent is a creative and how creative is an intelligent person?

The creative act, as we wrote in the previous chapter, is defined by 'effective surprise'. How can we investigate this process; how can we measure the ability to be creative or predict creative production? This problem falls into the province of scientific psychology and psychologists have wrestled with it for quite some time. Not being able to come to grips with the creative process as a whole, such as poets, artists and scientists have introspectively described it, psychologists have indulged in something of a sleight-of-hand and have fallen back on small segments of behaviour that are, on the face of it, integral parts of creativity and that, above all, are measurable. I will discuss below the difficulties involved in relying on what must to the layman appear as fragmentary, trivial tasks, as an approximation to creativity.

Whilst there have been attempts to measure fluency and other aspects of creative behaviour ever since the end of the nineteenth century, the topic fell into relative neglect and the revival of interest in it and what Hudson has called 'a boom in the American psychological industry' can be dated precisely and traced back to Guilford's 1950 paper on creativity. Through the careful studies of young adults of 'high-level ability', using modern measurement and correlational techniques which he originated at the Psychological Laboratory of the University of Southern California and through the ingenious and 'creative' tests which he suggested, he exerted a seminal influence on a whole movement of what has become known as 'creativity research'.

Origins of intelligence tests

Guilford's concern for probing the creative aspects of mental activity and for inventing new kinds of tests arose from deep-rooted dissatisfaction with the existing kinds of tests of achievement and general ability, especially as used in America. The system of testing has in fact frequently been identified with the whole approach to education:

> The present system is criticised for favouring the conformist mentality—the pupil or student who is good at accepting and learning what his teachers and lecturers tell him, and thinking and writing along conventional lines, whereas it discourages spontaneous, independent thought ... (Vernon, 1967b)

Guilford claimed that the traditional criterion for the construction of intelligence tests has been school achievement and therefore: 'Operationally, then, intelligence has been the ability to master reading and arithmetic and similar subjects. These subjects are not conspicuously demanding of creative talent' (Guilford, 1950).

This, however, is only a partial and somewhat distorted truth. Binet and Simon, whose intelligence test of 1905 started a 'boom' in psychology parallel to the present one in creativity, devised their test at the request of the Minister of Public Instruction in Paris, in order to identify children who not only had failed at school, but who were not likely to make adequate progress in the future. Teachers, they found, could, of course, pick out children who were failing, but included many who were simply 'lazy' or suffered from some temporary blockage. Binet and Simon's test, therefore, had to agree with the children's demonstrated school achievements or lack of them, but also had to go beyond these.

The test and all it derivatives with its, as Jensen (1969) points out, had their origins in the Paris schools of the 1900s and were implicitly shaped by the educational traditions of Europe and North America. We tend to take these traditions, with their goals and typical methods of instruction, and with their expectation of failure, so much for granted that it is difficult for us to imagine any different ones. The tests were designed to identify some of the basic skills prerequisite for success in such an educational system, such as ability to comprehend verbal input, to grasp relationships between things and their symbolic representations. Overall, despite all the criticism levelled at them, these tests have done their job reasonably well.

Mechanics of intelligence tests

At this stage it is necessary to explain shortly the statistical concept of 'correlation'. Say, a group of children take a test of language and a test of arithmetic and the rank order—purely hypothetically—is as in Table IA. We then say that the tests are perfectly correlated, since the first child in language is also the first child in arithmetic and so on down to the last child. Working it out mathematically we would arrive at a (positive) correlation of 1.0. If, by bad luck, the rank orders came out as in Table IB, we would have a perfect negative correlation, expressed mathematically as —1.0. These are purely fictitious examples, however. Much more typical would be rank orders as illustrated in Table IC. Here we see some correspondence between the two rank orders, since, for instance, the top three children in language are also the top three in arith-

Child	Language	Arithmetic

Rank orders

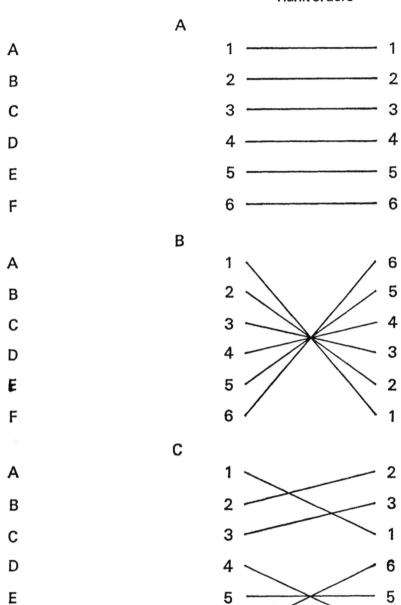

TABLE I Correlation of tests

metic and the bottom three children in language are also the bottom three in arithmetic, though the correspondence is by no means perfect. In mathematical terms this would yield a moderate degree of correlation, say 0.5 or 0.6. Correlation coefficients, then, vary between 1.0 and −1.0 and a correlation of 0 indicates that there is no discernible correlation or correspondence between the rank orders at all. In this way we can work out the correlation between any two tests and determine the overlap between them, but it should be said that, although we used rank orders for simplicity in the illustration, more often we correlate actual test scores.

Intelligence testing was refined and made more sophisticated by means of correlational techniques. Spearman, in the early 1900s, using these techniques, found a general factor running through all cognitive tests, which he labelled *g*. Furthermore, tests that seemed to correlate most highly with a battery of cognitive tests came to be chosen as the best indicators of 'intelligence', and they generally turned out to be tests of reasoning, abstraction or relational thinking.

At a later stage, then, intelligence was defined as 'more general thinking capacities' or as involving abstraction, conceptualization and problem-solving, and the criterion thus shifted from simple reading and arithmetic to the generality of cognitive tests with which any new intelligence test had to correlate.

The Binet-Simon Test and its direct descendants were individual, 'open-ended' tests in which the child had to supply the answers. However, in America after World War I with its Army Classification Test, testing became a large-scale industry with its attendant mechanization, and multiple-choice tests came to predominate for convenience in group testing. (A similar process, on a lesser scale, occurred in Britain.)

Some typical examples of the kind of test with which

readers will be familiar would be:

(a) Hand is to glove as foot is to ... (leg, arm, shoe, toe)
(b) Fill in the missing numbers: 2 4 6 ... 12 14 16
(c) Which is the odd man out? ... Chair, table, sideboard, settee, lamp.

It is true to say that between the wars very little was done to make these 'intelligence tests' broader, to introduce more adventurous content or a new format: they became stereotyped. For each item one correct answer has been predetermined; the tests are thus examples of the 'closed-system' thinking discussed in the first chapter. The 'testee's' task is to discover the answer that the examiner has keyed as correct and the possibility exists that more than one answer may be logically correct among the given alternatives, though this happens very rarely in well-constructed tests. It has been said, with some justification, that in such a case it will be the original mind that would pick on the remote, unexpected answer and would thereby be penalized. A not quite serious example—not, I hasten to add, taken from an actual intelligence test—might be the following:

Which is the odd man out?—Mat, wife, egg, sex.

The conventional person would reply: wife, because it is the only four-letter word. The original mind, however, might say: sex, because you can beat a mat, a wife and an egg. (In fact, 'mat' is another defensible answer, for reasons that the alert reader will discover for himself.)

The multiple-choice test does not provide an opportunity for creativeness, and, it has been claimed, may not pick out those who will be productive in later life. When it permeates the whole of school life, including the assessment of school attainments, it may well have a narrowing and mind-numbing effect. It was because he was aware and critical of the narrowness of the test format and of the abilities being tested that Guilford set out on his search for broader and different kinds of tests which would evoke such qualities as imagination, originality, or fluency and novelty of ideas.

Theory of the intellect

Guilford, however, did more than just devise some new tests: he placed them in a comprehensive theoretical framework, the *structure of intellect* model (Guilford, 1959). The bricks he used for building this model were 'factors' of the intellect that had already been identified plus others which he hypothesized and hoped to verify through further research. A 'factor' is found by correlating various tests with each other and determining mathematically which tests cluster together along certain dimensions, the dimensions, or 'factors' having been arrived at by the method of 'factor-analysis' (no relation of psycho-analysis, it should be stressed) (see Figure 1). A factor is thus essentially a cluster of tests which can be seen by inspection to have certain properties in common. Guilford and many other factor-analysts, however, go further and suggest that these test factors represent factors of the mind, but such a statement takes us beyond the direct evidence and must base its validity on circumstantial evidence and a certain measure of faith.

Guilford's 'structure of the intellect' consists of a classification of intellectual factors already discovered or still to be identified. The three-way classification which he employs is based on underlying aspects of tests and he has represented it by means of the model of a cube depicted in Figure 2.

One basis of classification is the kind of process or operation performed and Guilford distinguishes between five groups of abilities: the factors of cognition, memory, convergent thinking, divergent thinking, and evaluation. Here we return to the title of this chapter and find that 'convergent thinking' is essentially what we have previously

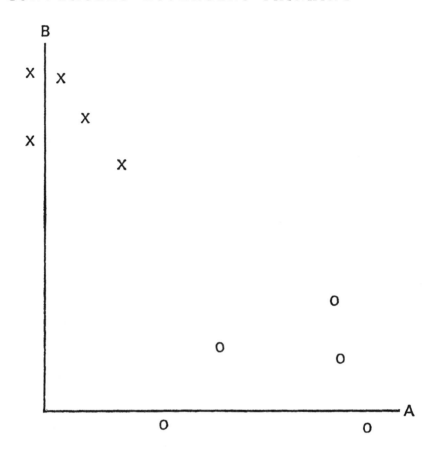

O – Tests that cluster or are 'highly loaded' on factor A, say 'convergent thinking'

X – Tests that cluster or are 'highly loaded' on factor B, say 'divergent thinking'

FIG. I

called 'closed-system thinking' and 'divergent thinking' corresponds roughly to 'adventurous thinking'. Guilford (1959) writes: 'In divergent-thinking operations we think in different directions, sometimes searching, sometimes seeking variety. In convergent thinking the information leads to

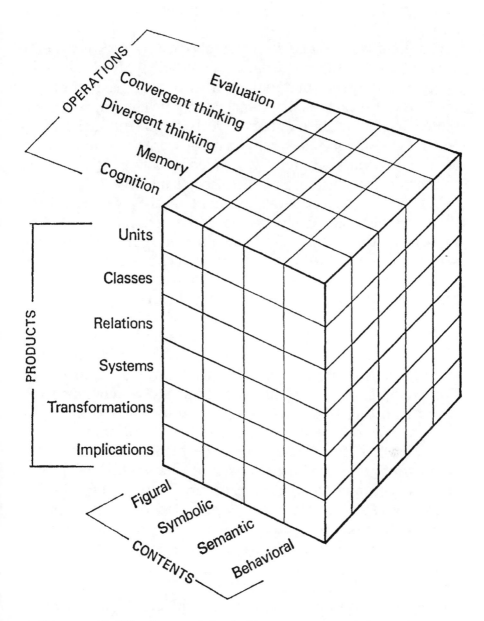

FIG. 2   Guilford's model of the structure of the intellect

one right answer or to a recognized best or conventional answer.'

A second way of classifying intellectual factors is according to the kind of material or content involved. Figural content is concrete material such as is perceived through the senses (e.g. shapes, diagrams). Symbolic content is represented by letters or numbers or other conventional signs. Semantic content takes the form of verbal meanings or ideas. Behavioural content was added on a theoretical basis to include what has been called 'social intelligence'.

When operations operate on content they generate the six types of products shown along the vertical axis of the model, the third basis of classification. The products represent ways of classifying ideas and concepts, or, as Guilford writes, 'they may serve as basic classes into which one might fit all kinds of information psychologically.'

Guilford has already filled well over half of the 120 cells of the model with named factors and is engaged in filling more. Tests will vary along all three dimensions simultaneously and can thus be fitted into particular cells. For example, the test of ideational fluency which calls for, say, the listing of objects that are round and edible fits into the cell 'divergent production of semantic units'.

One row of the model cube is devoted to the divergent production of transformations and the factor 'adaptive flexibility' can be thought of as occupying the figural cell in that row. This has typically been tested by 'match problems', a well-known game in which the person is asked to take away a given number of matches to leave a stated number of squares. He thus has to transform the figure in front of him and in one variation he is to produce two or more transformations for each problem. Figure 3 illustrates this test.

Transformation of semantic material involves producing shifts and changes of meaning and the more novel, unusual or 'clever' the shift, the greater the transformation accomplished. This factor has often been called 'Originality', and 'Plot Titles', in which the examinee is told to invent as many appropriate titles as possible for a given story, is a good test of it. One of Guilford's stories concerns a missionary who has been captured by cannibals in Africa. He is in the pot and about to be boiled when a princess of the tribe obtains a promise for his release if he will become her mate. He refuses and is boiled to death.

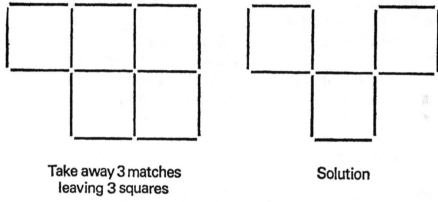

Take away 3 matches
leaving 3 squares

Solution

FIG. 3   Match problem test

In scoring the test the responses are divided into two categories, clever and non-clever. Examples of non-clever responses obtained by Guilford for this story are: African Death, Defeat of a Princess, Eaten by Savages, The Princess, The African Missionary, In Darkest Africa and Boiled by Savages. The number of such responses are counted as a score of ideational fluency. Examples of 'clever' responses are: Pot's Plot, Potluck Dinner, Stewed Parson, Goil or Boil, A Mate Worse than Death, He Left a Dish for a Pot, Chaste in Haste, and A Hot Price for Freedom. The number of clever responses is the score for originality, or the divergent production of semantic transformations.

Tests exist or have been devised also for other operations, e.g. cognition or convergent thinking, as well as other kinds of products. The important point about Guilford's view of the intellect is that he has identified factorially a multiplicity of intellectual abilities, even though other workers have detected a certain amount of overlap between them. For him the intellect is not monolithic, nor does it consist solely of convergent and divergent abilities, but it is multifaceted. He looks on it as an information-processing agency which deals with information of various kinds in a variety of ways.

Guilford's theories have evident implications for education, too. Learning for him 'is the discovery of information, not merely the formation of associations'. Education, he thinks, should train the child in the various ways of discovering, manipulating and transforming information, taking account of the variety of abilities that he possesses.

Whether Guilford's theory of the intellect will stand up in the light of further knowledge it is too early to say. However, it has certainly come out well by another touchstone by which any theory may be tested, namely that of fruitfulness for research. For many other toilers in the field of creativity have derived and adapted their tests from ideas proposed by Guilford and his collaborators, even if they did not follow the detailed factor specifications implied in the original theory.

'Intelligence' and 'creativity'

One topic that has preoccupied many psychologists who were impressed, but not quite convinced, by Guilford is: are 'intelligence' and 'creativity' really two distinct traits or would the concept of intelligence considered as a unitary trait encompass the creativity phenomenon within its broad folds? Since 'intelligence' has traditionally been largely measured by convergent tests (with the exception of some sub-tests of the Binet Scale), the question resolves itself into: are convergent and divergent tests measuring distinct traits? This question is of practical importance particularly if one's rating on intelligence, and therefore one's standing in the community or entry to certain professions, were to depend on one's performance on convergent tests alone. The technique of factor-analysis has been used to test whether convergent and divergent tests tend to cluster on several different factors. It is also possible to compare the magnitude of the correlations among divergent tests and among convergent tests separately with the size of the correlation between convergent and divergent tests. If these two types of test form two separate domains the correlation between them should be much lower than the correlations within each test battery.

One of the best-known researches that attempted to demonstrate the independence of the 'creativity' and 'intelligence' domains is that by Getzels and Jackson (1962). These writers used as their sample pupils in a private Chicago school who came predominantly from middle-class and professional homes and whose average IQ was 132. They then compared two contrasting groups: the 'high-lows' who came in the top 20 per cent on divergent tests, but were not in the top 20 per cent for IQ ('high creatives'), and the 'low-highs' who were in the top 20 per cent for IQ, but not for divergent thinking ('high IQs'). Some of the interesting contrasts they found between these groups will be discussed in later chapters. They also correlated the creativity measures among themselves and with IQ scores, using the whole of their sample for this. The correlations between single divergent tests and IQ averaged only 0·26 for boys but the correlations among divergent tests themselves were not much higher, averaging 0·28. This study has been severely criticized—with some justification—because in the first place their whole sample was so atypical and because they then chose for detailed investigation a minority of extreme cases, leaving out of account the majority who would, for instance, include the interesting group of 'high-highs'. It is difficult to remember at times that the group 'low' on intelligence had an average IQ of 127!

Hudson in England found correlations between his convergent and divergent tests similar to Getzels and Jackson's and he also formed two contrasting groups in a parallel way, but basing his distinction on bias of scores (i.e. relatively higher divergent than convergent scores and vice-versa) rather than on absolute levels (Hudson, 1966). In calling his groups 'convergers' and 'divergers' he also begged fewer questions than Getzels and Jackson did with their 'high' and 'low' creatives.

Hasan Butcher (1968) repeated part of the Getzels and Jackson study in Scotland on an unselected population and found considerably higher correlations between divergent tests and IQ so that they came to the conclusion that divergent tests are hardly distinguishable from convergent ones. However, most investigators who use factor-analytic techniques were in fact able to identify one or more factors on which divergent tests clustered, separable from a convergent thinking factor (e.g. Cropley, 1966, Vernon, 1967a, Dacey, Madaus and Allen, 1969). At the same time they all noted significant correlations between divergent and convergent tests and did not consider that the two factors were completely independent of one another.

Wallach and Kogan (1965) originated an invigoratingly novel approach to this whole question. Starting out from admitted disappointment with the generally established level of correlations between convergent and divergent tests they made the suggestion that this may have been due to the test-like atmosphere and pressure under which these measures were always administered. They therefore removed the evaluative atmosphere and time-pressure of school achievement and IQ tests from the situation, disguised their tests as 'games' and had the normal class-teacher give them during ordinary lesson time. (They were tests of ideational fluency and of uniqeness of ideas.)

The results were striking: the average correlation amongst the divergent tests was 0.4, amongst the intelligence and attainment measures 0.5 and the average correlation between these two sets of measures was 0.1. In this way they, too, established a divergent-thinking dimension to their satisfaction.

The hypothesis has been put forward that above a certain ability level—say IQ 120—creative capacities no longer depend on any further addition of IQ points and divergent and convergent thinking above this line are therefore essentially independent of each other. In the absence of a certain amount of general intelligence, however, no great creative production can occur either, so that in the lower reaches of ability the two modes of thought tend to vary in line with each other. This 'branching-tree theory' has been confirmed by some authors (e.g. Yamamoto, 1965, Haddon and Lytton, 1968), but not by others, though it remains a plausible one.

What is the upshot of all this? Hudson (1968) suggests that the poor intercorrelations among divergent tests may be explained by the tendency of divergers to be more wilful, idiosyncratic and fluctuating in the effort they put forth on divergent tasks. Differences between convergers and divergers in matters unconnected with the tests, such as personality, or home background, would tend to confirm the reality of the distinction. Overall, although convergent and divergent thinking clearly overlap, the evidence points to the existence of a domain of divergent thinking, distinct from conventional intelligence tests, as shown by differing factors. It is most illuminating, perhaps, to think of them as different styles of thought, as two complementary aspects of intellectual ability broadly conceived.

Do 'creativity tests' measure creativity?

The tests that serve the psychologist as tools in the study

of 'creativity' and in the dissection of the intellect can be seen to be but poor and trivial fragments of what they are trying to measure. Granted that they are only small segments of behaviour, do they even belong to the same class of product as the works of a Michelangelo, a Darwin, a Mozart—or a Beatle? Is it true that a future Leonardo da Vinci or Einstein can be picked out from the rest of us by his score on 'unusual uses' or 'match problems'? However, to apply such an ultimate standard of creativity to test the tests is an impracticable proposition, for it is by the work of a life-time that we judge such creative efforts and we achieve consensus on a man's creative eminence usually only some time after his death.

We have to be satisfied with different sorts of criteria and, indeed, divergent tests can be useful, if they identify more moderate degrees of creative potential. They certainly possess face validity, since we expect, say, 'originality' or the ability to transform to play an important part in original work. One way of discovering whether the tests identify real-life achievement has been to give them to architects, research scientists or others who had been rated on their creative abilities by their peers or superiors (see chapter 3). Generally their validity in such investigations turned out to be low, if not negligible. However, the failure to establish significant correlations between these criteria and the tests may be as much due to the deficiencies of the criteria as of the tests. There has generally been a lack of consistency in the criteria employed, e.g. MacKinnon (1962) rated architects by the publicity and prominence they had attained plus a five-point scale which included originality of thinking, ingenuity and the ability to set aside established conventions. Gough (1961), on the other hand, based ratings for his scientists on research competence, theoretical orientation, as well as original potential and general sophistication. The differences in these two examples are obvious, quite apart from the ambiguity inherent in some of the labels attached to the criteria. In some instances, also, the basis for making judgments on people's creative ability is rather slender, e.g. when teachers, whose knowledge of their pupils is confined to the classroom, are asked to provide ratings.

It has also been assumed too easily that creative people in all walks of life—painters, writers, scientists—could be tested on divergent tests with any content. Yet it is reasonable to expect that different kinds of content—figural, semantic, symbolic—would be applicable to different fields of activity. It is hardly surprising, therefore, that Beittel (1964) found no significant relationship when he correlated semantic test scores with criteria of creative performance of college art students, whereas Elliott (1964), using the same type of content, obtained a significant positive relationship with the creative ability of advertising and public relations personnel.

Some recent investigations have succeeded in establishing some sort of validity for divergent tests by relating them to pupils' concurrent extra-curricular activities, a less satisfactory criterion than real achievement over time, though it can be argued, as Wallach and Wing (1969) do, that 'nonacademic or extracurricular forms of talented accomplishments come closer to representing what accomplishment is like in the years after formal schooling is over than is the case for academic achievement.' These authors found that nonacademic talented accomplishments, such as signs of leadership (election to the presidency of the student government, etc.), talent in the visual arts (displaying pictures in an exhibition, or winning an award in a competition), expertise in literary activities (writing poetry for pleasure, etc.), extracurricular activity in science (constructing scientific apparatus, etc.), were strongly related to output of ideas or ideational productivity, but not so clearly to uniqueness of ideas, and were not related to intelligence status. To put the last point into proper perspective it must be stated that their subjects were students in a selective American college and hence were all in the upper reaches of general intelligence.

Dewing (1970) too found a positive relationship in an unselected group of twelve-year-olds in Australia between performance on the Minnesota Tests of Creative Thinking and a combination of outside criteria: a check list of extra-curricular activities, teacher ratings, peer ratings and imaginative writing.

The evidence, such as it exists, that divergent test scores are related to real-life creative performance is not very strong. In part this may be because personality factors, e.g. single-minded devotion to a field of work or nonconformist judgment, by common consent play an important role in creative work, whereas they are not represented in short, one-shot tasks. It would be simplistic to identify divergent thinking completely with creativity and yet much of the burgeoning literature assumes that divergent thinking equals creativity and creative persons are everything that is good, wholesome, humane and progressive. Convergers, by logical deduction, are the reverse. Yet, as Hudson (1966) has suggested, divergers tend to be interested in literature and the arts, and to specialize in these. Convergers, on the other hand, turn to science—and not all of them will be uncreative, humdrum scientists. In Hudson's study boys who were technically inventive—even those who were outstandingly so—performed poorly on divergent tests. Roe (1953), from her investigation, also reports that creative scientific researchers resemble convergers. We are therefore not entitled to conclude that only divergers will be productive in a real-life situation. The relation between divergent thinking and creativity in science and technology, in particular, is far more complex than this and our researches have not yet gone far in unravelling it.

42

3

What are creative people like?

Is the popular image of the creative person—in particular the artist—as a long-haired, sloppy, disorderly, Bohemian, half-mad individual correct? Both writers and psychologists have thought and written about what kind of man the creative person really is. Here is what Arthur Koestler, the writer, had to say about it:

Most geniuses responsible for the major mutations in the history of thought seem to have certain features in common; on the one hand scepticism, often carried to the point of iconoclasm, in their attitude towards traditional ideas, axioms, and dogmas, towards everything that is taken for granted; on the other hand, an openmindedness that verges on naïve credulity towards new concepts which seem to hold out some promise to their instinctive gropings. Out of this combination results that crucial capacity of perceiving a familiar object, situation, problem, or collection of data, in a sudden new light or new context: of seeing a branch not as part of a tree, but as a potential weapon or tool: of associating the fall of an apple not with its ripeness, but with the motion of the moon. The discoverer perceives relational patterns of functional analogies where nobody saw them before, as the poet perceives the image of a camel in a drifting cloud. (Koestler, 1959)

This is a literary person's view, intuitively convincing and certainly in line with Koestler's theory of the creative process. Psychologists, being pedestrian and literal-minded people, want to know the evidence for such propositions— and have gone to look for it.

The discussion in the last chapter has shown that research into the cognitive correlates of creative abilities has not provided all the answers. Indeed, looking on divergent thinking as merely a cognitive ability confines us to a limited view and there is a good case for arguing that until we also take personality variables into account, further clarification of the creativity dimension will elude us. One of the potential benefits of research into divergent thinking in fact is that it may breach the walls between cognitive and non-cognitive psychology, between research into personality and into mental abilities—and has, in fact, done so.

Creative men

Indeed, a great deal has already been done in trying to elucidate what personal qualities, what background make a person creative. A combination of idiographic methods, i.e. the study of individuals, and nomothetic methods, i.e. the large-scale study of groups, is probably best suited to this purpose and both types have been applied in this endeavour. Let us start with what has been discovered about adults.

One of the earliest investigations in the modern style into the personality and background of scientists, selected because they were eminent, was carried out by Roe (1952). Her twenty biologists, twenty-two physicists and twenty-two social scientists (psychologists and anthropologists) were chosen by panels of experts in their respective fields. Roe then subjected them to long interviews covering their life history, family background, professional and recreational interests, ways of thinking etc. as well as to intelligence tests and clinical personality tests (Rorschach ink blots and Thematic Apperception Test) which probed their inner preoccupations and attitudes to themselves and the world around them, in short their personality structure.

While, naturally, every scientist displayed his own individuality, and while differences emerged between the different professional groups, common patterns could also be detected and Roe ventured to draw a picture of the 'average' eminent scientist—almost a contradiction in terms.

> He was the first-born child of a middle-class family, the son of a professional man. He is likely to have been a sickly child or to have lost a parent at an early age. He has a very high IQ and in boyhood began to do a great deal of reading. He tended to feel lonely and 'different' and to be shy and aloof from his classmates. He had only a moderate interest in girls and did not begin dating them until college. He married late (at 27), has two children and finds security in family life; his marriage is more stable than the average. Not until his junior or senior year in college did he decide on his vocation as a scientist. What decided him (almost invariably) was a college project in which he had occasion to do some independent research—to find out things for himself. Once he discovered the pleasure of this kind of work, he never turned back. He is completely satisfied with his chosen vocation. (Only one of the 64 eminent scientists—a Nobel prize winner—says he would have preferred to do something else: he wanted to be a farmer, but could not make a living at it.) He works hard and devotedly in his laboratory, often seven days a week. He says his work is his life and he has few recreations, those being restricted to fishing, sailing, walking or some other individualistic activity. The movies bore him. He avoids social affairs and political activity, and religion plays no part in his life or thinking. Better than any other interest or activity, scientific research seems to meet the inner need of his nature. (Roe, 1952)

Some of the differences between the groups throw a revealing light on the inner motives that may have impelled each into his chosen field (apart from the college project mentioned above). The biologists and physicists showed considerable independence from their parents and suffered no guilt feelings about this, whereas the social scientists had on the one hand dependent attitudes towards their parents, but on the other were also rebellious and demonstrated concern about interpersonal relationships generally. It was the social scientists, too, who were the most aggressive and the biologists the least.

One of the factors about these scientists that impressed Roe most was their independence of mind and she saw signs of this in the fact that they liked best teachers who let them alone, in their attitude towards religion and personal relations and in their satisfaction in a career in which they were left largely to their own direction and decisions. We shall see later some of these factors reappear in other research.

The most comprehensive and convincing network of findings on the personality of men and women who have creative achievements to their credit comes from Berkeley, from research done at the Institute for Personality Assessment and Research, (IPAR), chiefly by MacKinnon, Barron and Gough. These men used the bold design of asking the great and not so great to come to the Institute for an assessment week-end, where they actually lived in for two to three days together with the assessment staff. MacKinnon had experience of this broad-sweep assessment of men through his work in the war-time U.S. Office of Strategic Services where a similar plan was employed for assessing and selecting men for dangerous and secret missions.

The chief research at the Institute was done on creative architects, writers and mathematicians. An important preliminary task was to ensure the selection of the really creative and eminent, to be contrasted with more ordinary specimens of their profession. In each field experts, e.g. five professors of architecture in the case of the architects, were asked to nominate the most creative people working in their field. Those receiving most nominations from the experts were invited to come to Berkeley for the week-end of tests and assessments. However, it is easier to gain the voluntary co-operation of devoted men for such an enterprise in war-time than it is to enlist in peace-time the collaboration of the famous for their own dissection, when it is not at all clear to them that the work is *pro bono publico*. There were some rather testy refusals and one of the consenting victims, after the experience, ventured to dissect the dissectors in a satirical piece in the *Nation*, called 'The Vivisection of a Poet' (Rexroth, 1957). However, it appears that those who came (forty architects for instance) co-operated with the project.

The less creative workers were chosen by locating in lists or directories of their profession, say, forty architects who were identical in age and geographical location with the eminent architects first selected. Various checks ensured that the 'creative' workers were really more creative and productive than the more representative members of their professions. However, the representative architects and writers did not participate in the living-in assessments, but answered tests and questionnaires by mail. This somewhat detracts from the symmetry and the comprehensiveness of the study.

Each session assembled together between five and ten distinguished practitioners of their respective professions, together with a bevy of psychologists and psychiatrists. Various formal tests and assessments were administered, but the total group also lived together for three days in comfort, if not luxury, something which provided opportunities for conversations and direct observation of normal, everyday behaviour. At the end of the assessment period the psychologists wrote down their impressions of each subject and characterized each by choosing the most appropriate adjectives from a long adjective check list.

They also described the subjects in sentences of somewhat more technical and clinical import. To integrate this direct information into a full picture of the individual a 'case conference' of all staff members was also held. This intuitive kind of summing-up was achieved without knowledge of the test results and was based simply on the observed actions and words of the participants.

The results of this procedure are not easily assembled and compared, as they are scattered over several publications, not all of which are easily accessible (e.g. MacKinnon *et al.* 1961, MacKinnon, 1962, Gough, 1961), and the presentation at times lacks something in clarity, nor have all the findings yet been completely analysed. The most coherent account, on which the following is largely based, can be found in Barron (1969). Different groups of professionals were given slightly different selections of tests and assessments and this, together with the fact, already noted, that some groups received their tests and questionnaires at home by mail, makes the drawing of full and clear conclusions a somewhat hazardous affair.

The prominence given in the literature to the study of architects is not accidental. Architects as a profession, after all, have to combine in their work, if they are to be successful, the aesthetic sensibility of the artist who tries to please and to delight, with the technical efficiency, the know-how and the practicality of the engineer and scientist who has to make sure that his products stand up to use in the workaday world. It was, therefore, thought that the architect is the prototype of the artist-scientist and that it might be assumed that the qualities he displays—if he is creative—form, as it were, the common denominator of creative qualities *per se*. However, the traits and qualities actually found among creative workers differ somewhat as between the different professional groups. Let me start with those that are common to architects and writers, and to some extent to mathematicians.

In the staff descriptions, both by means of adjectives and by means of sentences (Clinical Q-sort Items), creative workers as a group appear as outstandingly intelligent and imaginative; they show a trait of individualism and independence which enables them to go their own way to achieve their aspirations which generally tend to be high. At the same time they display a self-centredness which is perhaps a necessary ingredient of high achievement and finally, as you might expect, they enjoy artistic impressions and show aesthetic sensibilities. Writers and architects, but not mathematicians, were described as productive and able to get things done, as having a wide range of interests and as valuing intellectual and cognitive matters. (This last is a rather surprising omission for distinguished mathematicians and one wonders about the fallibility of 'impressions'.)

Apart from staff descriptions, what do the personality tests have to tell us about the traits of these distinguished men and women? The evidence on neurosis and psychopathology, derived from an inventory measuring clinical abnormalities, will be discussed at a later stage. The subjects also took the California Psychological Inventory whose scales measure qualities indicative of 'ego-strength'. (These are qualities of robustness and stability, demonstrating that the rational, conscious part of the personality is in control and in effective touch with reality: examples are given below.) All three creative professional groups are well above the population norm, as well as above their less creative confrères in terms of the ability to achieve through independence rather than through conformity, in the qualities which underlie and lead to the achievement of social status, in being psychologically minded, i.e. open to other people's feelings, and in being possessed of more feminine interests. This last result (not applicable to the women mathematicians) having been repeated on several other tests assumes an air of definiteness and incontrovertibility, rare in psychological findings. It means that creative men have sensitivities and abilities which in our culture generally tend to be attributed to women (sensitivity to others' feelings may be one of them). In their sexual identifications and awareness they are more open and give more expression to the feminine side of their nature (since we all combine aspects of both sexes) than do professional workers in general. MacKinnon (1962) indeed indicates that for some of these men the balance between masculine and feminine traits, interests and identification was a precarious one, achieved only after great psychic stress and turmoil. Another trait in which the creatives are uniformly high, and women mathematicians outstandingly so, is flexibility, but this has ramifications to be discussed below.

Creative architects and writers also tend to be dominant, to be capable of interacting effectively in a social setting, though they are not particularly sociable, and they show self-confidence and self-assurance, all qualities which the eminent women mathematicians do not share.

It is of interest to note, too, the qualities on which all three professional groups obtained a low score: they are all, in one way or another, connected with social conformity. Thus the creative men and women are below par in sociability, in self-control, in the values inculcated by traditional socialization, i.e. they are comparatively free from conventional restraints and inhibitions. They show this again by the absence of desire to make a good impression and by their readiness to challenge commonly held views.

Some very interesting results were achieved with a test (the Myers-Briggs Type Indicator) which is based on Carl G. Jung's typology of personality. One of the contrasts here is between the judging and the perceptive type. 'A judging type places more emphasis upon the control and regulation of experience, while a perceptive type is inclined to be more open and receptive to all experience.' Mac-

Kinnon found that the majority of creative architects, writers and mathematicians were perceptive types. Another contrast measured by this Indicator is a preference between two different types of perception: sensation, i.e. direct perception through the senses, and intuition, which transcends immediate appearances to reach deeper meanings and possibilities implied in things and situations. While in the general population 25 per cent show a preference for the intuitive style, this was the preferred style of over 90 per cent of creative writers, mathematicians and scientists, and of actually 100 per cent of the architects.

Another well-known personality distinction based on Jung's typology is that between introverts and extroverts. It is in accord with and corroborates some of the findings quoted earlier, that MacKinnon found approximately two-thirds of all his creative groups to be on the introverted side of the balance.

In commenting on the intuitive preference of the creatives MacKinnon writes: 'One would expect creative persons not to be bound to the stimulus and the object, but to be ever alert to the as-yet-not-realized.' This is the trait at times called *openness to experience* and evidence for its prominence amongst creative persons has been found in several investigations. An interesting demonstration of the role it plays was provided by an experiment (Mendelssohn and Griswold, 1966) in which students were given a printed list of words to learn and had another set of tape-recorded words played to them as interference. Afterwards they were asked to solve some simple anagrams, but they were not told that the solutions to some of the anagrams had been contained in the printed list and some in the interference list of words. Those who had on another test been shown to be high creatives solved more of the anagrams for which they had indirectly been given the answers. Their attention somehow embraced a part of their experience that others found irrelevant and this 'openness' is what characterizes creative persons, whether the experience is in the recent or in the long distant past. In a similar vein Barron writes of men of letters being open to mystic experiences, to feelings of awe and oneness with the universe.

On the debit side of the balance sheet 'openness to experience' may also bring with it a certain credulity and ingenuousness, something on which Koestler, for instance (see quotation on page 43), has remarked. A recent study (McHenry and Shouksmith, 1970) has, indeed, found divergent ten-year-olds to be suggestible, in that divergent ability was significantly associated with yielding to the supposed majority interpretation of inkblots, where this interpretation was patently inappropriate and ran counter to the individual's previous ideas.

This stands in stark contrast to the independent-mindedness of creative individuals attested to by various studies, e.g. Cattell and Drevdahl (1955), Crutchfield (1962) and also by a group pressure study similar to the above, carried out at the IPAR. Barron found that in a task of estimating lines, given to his group of architects and writers, creative ability was significantly correlated with greater independence of judgment, i.e. with less willingness to yield to the majority opinion. Perhaps it was these persons' very eminence that provided them with a buffer of self-assurance and hence independence? For being suggestible also enables the creative person to absorb new and perhaps improbable ideas from his surroundings and would therefore seem to be a useful trait. The contradiction is not easy to resolve.

Flexibility was one of the attributes for which creative writers, architects and mathematicians were outstanding and this quality—partly cognitive in nature—has been studied in the thought processes of creatively gifted individuals. Koestler has written of the 'games of the underground' where the mind temporarily relinquishes rational control over thought and reverts to a more primitive, dream-like process. In psycho-analytic language this latter is called primary process thinking, as opposed to secondary process which consists of rational conscious thought. It has been suggested that creative flexibility consists precisely in being able to 'regress' from normal secondary processes to primary ones and then return to secondary process thinking once again and in this way combine the two modes of thought, a shift for which Kris has coined the term 'regression in the service of the ego'. This has been investigated by means of personality tests and it seems that what matters for creative people is not so much the amount of primary process thinking that they indulge in, but the effectiveness with which they control it, in other words the use to which they put uninhibited, wild fantasy. An interesting elaboration of this concept comes from a study by Wild (1965), who contrasted art students with teachers and schizophrenics. (She did not want to imply, I think, that teachers are completely uncreative, but merely that they are less inclined and less trained for original productive work than art students.) Given Word Association and Object Sorting Tests the art students were indeed able to shift from responding in the manner of a 'regulated', cautious person to responding in the manner of an 'unregulated', whimsical person more easily than were either teachers or schizophrenics (the latter, incidentally, gave the fewest pathological responses). The result would seem to be consistent with the concept of 'regression in the service of the ego', as playing a part in the thinking processes of creative persons, though not with accepted ideas about schizophrenics.

A variable that proved highly distinctive of all creative groups in the IPAR researches was a preference for *perceptual complexity*, which perhaps lies only half in the personality domain. The groups were shown abstract line drawings in black and white which ranged from simple, clear geometrical shapes, e.g. semi-circles, regular poly-hedra etc. to drawings which appear to be childish scrawls and scribbles. Eighty American painters who had first been given this test showed a marked preference for the complex, asymmetrical and what they called 'vital' and 'dynamic' shapes. Equally, for the groups of professionals at Berkeley a preference for the complex, asymmetrical was correlated with creativity and for a group of research scientists it even turned out to be the best predictor of their rated productive powers. It would seem that creative persons are able to accept perceptual complexity and even disorder without being disturbed by it and actually prefer the richness of this complexity to the relative poverty of a simplified geometrical design. Since this Art Scale discriminates so consistently between creatives and non-creatives in all fields, it may, in fact, be a more useful means of identifying creatives than the more verbal Guilford-type paper-and-pencil tests.

The creative groups also showed a distinct hierarchy of values on the Allport-Vernon Lindzey Study of Values, the most important ones for them being the theoretical and the aesthetic. The authors of this scale believed there was some incompatibility between theoretical values, being directed at the discovery of rationality and truth, and aesthetic values which have beauty as their highest expression. Perhaps it is a distinguishing mark of creative individuals, as MacKinnon suggests, to be able to reconcile such contradictions within their own personalities.

We have reviewed a number of personality attributes that creative writers, mathematicians and architects, as well as possibly other professions, seem to have in common. We may, at least tentatively, consider these as distinctive of the creative individual as such. What about differences between the different groups? Some of the descriptions applied to writers and architects by the Berkeley staff can give us some clues. Creative writers, but not architects, were thought to be especially verbally fluent, to be concerned with philosophical problems, and to 'think and associate to ideas in unusual ways'. Architects, on the other hand, are business men, deal with materials as well as people and therefore have to be socially at ease and dependable. Hence, it is not surprising that a typical architect would be described as 'enjoys sensuous experiences', 'has social poise and presence; appears socially at ease', 'is a genuinely dependable and responsible person'.

Creative mathematicians, on the other hand, were not seen as having their feet on the ground, for they were not credited with being able to get things done, and not at all with being dependable and responsible (more average mathematicians were that). Far from being socially at ease they were described as courageous and original, but also as emotional—a portrayal which conjures up the picture of a somewhat maladroit eccentric.

Scientists were not included among the groups of professionals who came to Berkeley for the week-ends of tests and conversation, but a separate study on them was carried out by Gough (1961), using some of the same tests as for the other groups. R. B. Cattell also investigated eminent scientists, but by an approach rather different from the open-ended, clinical procedures employed at Berkeley. He used the psychometrically more tight-knit method of a questionnaire (the Sixteen Personality Factor Questionnaire) which he had devised and standardized and validated by means of factor analysis. In spite of the differences in methods there is a striking convergence of results.

The Berkeley study noted for eminent scientists characteristics that were quite similar to those of creative workers in other fields, such as high intelligence, a strong tendency towards independent judgment and achievement in independent ways, personal dominance, responsiveness to other people's interests and motives, i.e. psychological-mindedness, and a marked preference for aesthetic elegance and complexity of design.

Here again it seems that the impulse to creativity in science derives from the same forces in the dynamics of the person as creativity in other fields, yet there are also significant differences: whereas the other creators tended to be perceptual rather than judging in terms of Jung's personality types, creative research scientists were the reverse, thus stressing the commitment to the control and regulation of phenomena inherent in their profession. For research scientists, too, theoretical values (in the Study of Values), representing the search for truth and rationality, had precedence over aesthetic ones. It seems scientists, even creative ones, tend somewhat more towards the convergent types of thinking than creators in other fields.

Cattell's contribution (Cattell and Drevdahl, 1955) has some interesting additions to offer to this picture of creative scientists. He, like the IPAR study, found them highly intelligent, independent of mind and dominant, as well as sensitive in a psychological sense. But, in addition, his test showed that in relation to the average of the population these scientists were introspective, reserved and cool, that they tended to be outwardly inhibited, serious and taciturn and self-sufficient to a degree. Although it is notable that they were not—unlike artists, given the same test—outstandingly bohemian, nevertheless the image presented of the scientists denotes a fine disregard of social pleasantries as well as conventions, nicely illustrated by the story Cattell quotes about Lord Cavendish. When asked to attend a formal, perhaps rather starchy, social gathering arranged for visiting foreign scientists at Cambridge, he broke away and ran down the corridor 'squeaking like a bat'.

Young creatives

In selecting 'creative' children and adolescents for study we cannot rely on achievements or eminence: 'creativity' here has to be defined by high scores on tests of divergent thinking, with all the qualifications that this implies. So in talking about the personalities of 'young creatives' we are speaking of the personalities of 'divergers', as opposed to 'convergers', such as, for instance, Getzels and Jackson (1962) have studied. (It will be recalled that Getzels and Jackson called their divergers 'high creatives'—those who came in the top 20 per cent on divergent tests but not on IQ tests—and their convergers 'high IQs'—those who came in the top 20 per cent on the IQ tests, but not on divergent tests.)

Some of the personality characteristics of eminent men reappear among the young who show creative promise. Getzels and Jackson found that their divergers took a stand against the dominant values of their culture, thus showing unconventionality and independence of judgment. They were not interested in the qualities that make for worldly success, which their teachers esteemed, they rather prized qualities that were of value to them as persons, whilst fully realizing that these would not necessarily earn respect in the world. They also showed their unconventional bent in the kind of career they aspired to. Getzels and Jackson saw them essentially as outsiders in a school system that was made for a different type of child. Hence, in spite of their high school achievements, the 'high creatives' were slightly less popular with their teachers than were the 'high IQ' children. A very interesting difference between the divergers and convergers was the marked discrepancy in their parents' occupations. The convergers had very largely professional, university-trained parents, whereas the divergers came predominantly from a business background. One is compellingly reminded here of the occupational distinction between 'entrepreneur' and 'bureaucrat' which Miller and Swanson (1958) found was reflected in different attitudes of parents, especially to risk-taking (entrepreneurs taking more risks) and hence also produced differential effects on the children.

Humour and playfulness are two of the qualities by which the adolescents in Getzels and Jackson's study set most store and for which they were most outstanding. These qualities permeated not only their imaginative productions, but also their autobiographies. The beginning of a life story illustrates this:

> A shriek rang through the hall of the hospital. It was the nurse. In the process of being born, I had kicked her in the stomach. I was very little and round and red. I am no longer red or round, but I am still little.
>
> As a nursery-school child I was bashful. While the other children romped and played I hung back in the corner. The teacher tried to make me join the happy throng and I took a bite out of her ankle. Ah, my carefree childhood ... Surprisingly enough I have lived up to this age. (Getzels and Jackson, 1962, p. 190)

Getzels and Jackson noted their divergers were somewhat less popular with their teachers because of their nonconforming ways. Another American educator (Torrance, 1962) also suggested that the creative child will be lacking in popularity and that social pressures may be a factor inhibiting the development of divergent abilities. This may well be so in a society that puts a high value on conformity (something no doubt true of parts of both British and American society, of some British and some American schools). However, one could argue that qualities associated with divergency may also be qualities which make for good social relationships in a society in which originality is valued. Indeed, there is evidence that popularity as measured by a sociometric test is positively related to divergent thinking ability, particularly in progressive or 'informal' schools, whereas in more traditional 'formal' schools popularity is more closely associated with convergent ability (Haddon and Lytton, 1968).

Some of the personality ramifications of convergent and divergent thinking have been explored by Hudson (1966, 1968) in an interesting way. He found that convergers tended to adopt attitudes that are generally called 'authoritarian', i.e. convergers show respect of authority, are ready to accept expert advice, are more likely than divergers to approve of being obedient and tend to have set opinions. A corollary of this is that their rigidity makes them uncomfortable with the natural ambiguities in the world around them which they would prefer to resolve into black and white certainties. They are also less irked by a school syllabus and more 'syllabus-bound'. One would suspect the converger also to be more tidy and orderly, even 'obsessional', than the diverger. Yet, in fact, divergers reported themselves to be as orderly and methodical in their work habits as did convergers. But then, Dickens, too, was extraordinarily tidy, though remarkably productive and inventive—a far cry from the stereotype of the disorderly, scruffy artist.

Hudson has made some provocative suggestions regarding the underlying dynamics of divergent and convergent thinking which he considers as two contrasting styles of 'defence'. The converger shies away from dealings with people, from personal emotions and devotes his energies and thought to impersonal things and objects. In a sense he seeks refuge there from the turmoil that personal involvement with people would cause in him. He is also ultra-cautious in expressing his feelings, because for him they are dangerous territory that he is wary of entering. 'The converger uses some sort of mental barrier against thoughts and feelings which unsettle him. And the use of such barriers seems to secure him an area of security, within which he is free to pursue his interests, unhampered by emotional disruption' (Hudson, 1966).

This idea of the converger being on guard against feelings and unsettling thoughts that might well up within him

59

makes sense of his desperate desire to be conventional, of the conformist attitudes he adopts about many issues, of the rigidity and the compartmentalization of his thinking. All these are methods by which he defends himself against the anxiety aroused by the unusual and the conflictive. To ward off this anxiety he resorts to constrictions that will render him more secure.

All this has been commonly accepted amongst writers influenced by psycho-analytic thought. With it has gone the implication that it is an unhealthy reaction to the stresses of life, suggestive of poor adjustment. The diverger, on the other hand, who displays the opposite tendencies, has been credited with a healthy, wholesome, well-adjusted attitude. Hudson questions this and wonders whether the diverger's willingness to express his emotions and to revel in personal relations does not also conceal some weakness. Is this flaunting, this easy revelation of emotions not designed to cover up their essential shallowness? For some convergent thinking may well be an attempt to escape from anxiety about involvement with emotions and with people. On the other hand, the supposition that the converger's avoidance of the personal must *always* be a denial of emotion and a defence is based on an *a priori* scale of values that places letting oneself go above self-control and that accords a natural pre-eminence to concern with the personal—a psychologists' fallacy. Some individuals' interest in the physical world around them may, after all, be as natural and undistorted an expression of personality as other persons' interest in people. Moreover, the implied classification of convergers as second-rate intellects can be rather misleading, for they too can produce considerable achievements, e.g. in science, logic or mathematics. We are reminded, for instance, of the philosopher Kant, who wrote only works of precise logic, metaphysics and mathematics and by whose daily walk at noon, exactly, the good people of Koenigsberg used to set their watches.

Madness and genius

In the last section there emerged a view of convergers—often held by psychologists—as defensive, inhibited, even maladjusted individuals. The complementary view of divergers is that of persons who, to the extent that they are creative, open to experience, and uninhibited, display a calendar of virtues—wholesomeness, good adjustment, self-actualizing, power. A corollary claim is sometimes made that if only we could rid ourselves of our inhibitions how much more creative we could all be (cf. Kubie, 1958).

How far do such views mirror a verifiable reality, or do they oversimplify a complex situation? What about the opposite, popular view, represented by Dryden's famous lines:

> Great wits are sure to madness near allied
> And thin partitions do their bounds divide.
>
> *(Absalom and Achitophel)*

The evidence is but frail. We have Terman's *Genetic Studies of Genius* (1926-59) which followed children with IQs of more than 140 into adulthood and mid-life and which concluded quite definitely that high gifts were associated with greater than normal stability, as well as health, rather than the other way round. However, the definition of 'genius' as those with high IQ is a narrow one and while it may cover a great many successful people, it does not single out those with high creative gifts. So one is left with some doubts.

It is easy to compile a list of famous creators who showed severe psychotic or neurotic traits, or who lived such eccentric, rebellious or tumultuous lives that one must suspect their stability. Amongst musicians there were Beethoven and Bartok, amongst writers Henry James,

Rimbaud, Nietzsche, Proust or Eugene O'Neill, amongst painters one finds perhaps the most striking instability, e.g. in Van Gogh and even amongst scientists, such as Kepler, Darwin, Newton, one finds traits that are highly suggestive of psychological illness. However, such illustrations are no proof of a general trend: it would be just as easy to produce an even longer list of famous men who seem to have been perfectly stable and balanced.

We must now return to the Berkeley study of creative architects, writers and mathematicians, and consider the evidence this provides about their subjects' mental health or illness ('psychopathology' is the scientific jargon for the latter). This study included as one of its tests the Minnesota Multiphasic Personality Inventory which provides evidence on such psychiatric conditions as depression, hypochondriasis, hysteria, psychopathic deviation, paranoia, psychasthenia (neurosis) etc. The creative groups consistently showed greater psychopathology on all these scales than the more representative members of their professions. The average creative writer was in fact in the top 15 per cent of the general population for all these measures. The creative architect was a little less deviant, but still substantially above the mean for the general population. However, these men were not inmates of mental hospitals, but were eminent in their professions and had high achievements to their credit. They must therefore somehow have turned their weaknesses into strengths and woven their psychological difficulties into the fabric of their lives in such a way that they became part and parcel of their productive powers. In fact, the quality of 'ego strength' which enabled them to do this (already alluded to earlier) was also shown on another measure of the MMPI. While in the general population high scores on the pathological scales go with low scores on the ego-strength scale, these creative workers had as high scores on the ego-strength scale as they had on the others. They combined psychological stress with great personal effectiveness, a very unusual pattern, and—who knows?—the one may even have been the source of the other.

It is difficult therefore to deny that there is more than a chance association between psychiatric difficulties and creative powers, though this does not, of course, apply to each and every creative person. Nor is it probably a mere accident that this connection has been found more in the case of writers and artists than in that of other professions. Creative writers and artists constantly in their work confront and have to grapple with the boundaries of sanity in themselves, as well as in others, for their own personalities and experiences are the raw material of their craft. Lionel Trilling (1955) argues very convincingly against the idea that creative power must of necessity arise from suffering, that literary force must grow from 'sacrificial roots'. It is true, too, that inner conflicts do not by themselves make an artist any more than does the consumption of psychedelic drugs. Far more is required: 'What marks the artist is his power to shape the material of pain we all have' (Trilling, 1955). One is reminded of O'Neill who, in *Long Day's Journey into Night*, distilled the pain that overshadowed his life into a work of art, and whose *Desire under the Elms* can perhaps be regarded as the autobiography of his 'unconscious'. Yet, when Trilling suggests that artists only seem more wracked by conflicts and neurosis than creative scientists, because artists reveal their personality and their unconscious in their work, while scientists conceal it, we wonder. Perhaps it is because the scientist is more bound up with the material world and the need to control it, perhaps because he is more under the sway of everyday reality and all its trivia that he seems, on the whole, more stable. Whatever the reason, we have evidence that this is so: Cattell and Drevdahl (1955) showed that their scientists were marked by stability and Cox in her biographical studies (Terman *et al.*, 1926) described the scientists as 'the strongest and most forceful and best balanced (group) in the study'.

While it should be obvious that not every creative writer or artist is a sufferer of neurotic disabilities, nor every creative scientist completely free from them, the evidence seems to support the popular view that creative writers and artists tend to be subject to greater psychological perturbations than the average man. The question that has therefore sometimes been asked—and often by artists themselves—is whether their inner conflicts are so much bound up with their creativity that seeking to alleviate the anguish would destroy the creative powers, too. The artist here is in a dilemma: he feels burdened and constricted by his neurosis and may desperately desire to be liberated from it, yet any psychotherapeutic help, he fears, if effective, may free him of his chains but also, by stripping him of the source of his fertility, turn him into a vegetable. We do not know the answer to this question in any definite way, all we can do is speculate.

It may be that some artists, through psychotherapy, become reconciled to the fact that their talent is insufficient and ineffective for really creative work, but then the reason will be that the creative stream did not flow deeply in them, not that psychotherapy has made it any shallower; and a turn to some other more satisfactory mode of life will be felt as a relief. The case is different if the creative urge is deep-rooted. Then, as Storr (1968), himself an analyst, writes: 'We all have to express our own natures in life as we live it, and if art is part of a valid way of expressing ourselves it will not be destroyed.'

Paradoxically, opposition to psychotherapy out of fear that it may extinguish the creative fire is based on too sanguine a view of the power and efficacy of psychotherapy. The belief that it is a powerful agent of change that brings about a 'cure' of mental illness and changes people's personalities is nowadays hardly held by any person informed in this field, nor is such a claim made even by analysts. Rather than look on psychotherapy—or, more narrowly, psycho-analysis—as a method of 'cure', one does better to see it, in common with Storr (1968), as a form of semantic interpretation, which offers the patient a scheme that makes sense of his distress and, in doing so, alleviates it to some extent.

Perceived in this manner, psychotherapy cannot possibly spell danger to the artist. Viewed optimistically it might change his view of himself, give him greater insight into himself and hence into others and thereby enlarge his sympathy with other men. But his worst fears are not likely to be realized. However, all this is speculation, though I hope it is reasonable, for evidence on the effects of psychoanalysis on artists or writers is hard to find. On the other hand some modern writers give indications of considerable familiarity with analytical concepts—whether acquired by reading or by personal experience of analysis—and show insights in the delineation of character suggesting that psycho-analytic thought has affected the frame of reference within which they think and has thus enhanced their creative powers.

To end our consideration of this topic I will let some creative writers speak for themselves and they—rightly or wrongly—have more often felt that there was but a thin line between their powers of creation and the forces of unreason. Thus C. G. Jung writes, concerning the 'otherness' of artists: 'There are hardly any exceptions to the rule that a person must pay dearly for the divine gift of the creative fire' (Jung, 1933). Thomas Mann, himself, it would seem, one of the most reasonable and stable of writers, has devoted a book, *Doktor Faustus* (1967), to the conflict between sanity and genius. In it he writes (p. 237):

> Do you believe in genius that has nothing to do with hell? Non datur! The artist is the brother of the criminal and of the madman. Do you imagine any work of art

has ever been wrought without its maker learning to understand the way of the criminal and the lunatic? What is sick, what healthy? Without sickness life has never managed to survive!

4

Nurturing creativity

Home background

If we sum up—and oversimplify—the personality profiles of creative people that emerge from the research discussed in the last chapter, we can say that they are fiercely independent, unconventional and dominant, yet open to experience and flexible; that they show single-minded devotion to their work and destiny, prefer complex stimulation to simpler, orderly perception and display feminine interests, humour and playfulness.

How did creative individuals grow to be what they are? Since environmental forces play an important part in moulding the individual, can we find out which influences in their environment helped to produce creative persons? In this chapter we will be concerned with the parents that rear them and the culture that surrounds them, as well as with special training procedures; in the next chapter we will deal with the impact which school and college as institutions have on them.

As illustrations of families of convergers and divergers let me take the Scotts and the Blacks that appear in Getzels and Jackson's study (1962). The Scotts' daughter was one of the high IQ sample in that research, and finally attended a highly respected university in the Eastern United States.

The Scotts' apartment displays the impeccable taste to be expected of upper middle-class intellectuals and everything in it—furniture, books, etc.—is neat and orderly.

Mr Scott is a successful professional, but does not play a dominant role in the family. Lois's mother says that she, rather than the father, was responsible for rules and regulations in the household and that she was rather more rigid, but also more consistent, than he was. Mrs Scott feels justifiably proud of her daughter and gives her strong support in her ambitions for intellectual achievement, which she is, incidentally, fully capable of realizing. Throughout Lois's school career, from kindergarten to high school, Mrs Scott felt dissatisfied with what she considered to be the school's excessive emphasis on social adjustment at the expense of academic achievements. In fact, she wrote a special note to Lois's kindergarten, criticizing this aspect, although she concedes the emphasis has been changing slowly over the years since then. To assist Lois to achieve the standards of excellence that Mrs Scott considers essential she applies regular surveillance and sometimes even pressure, for instance, expecting a daily report about school activities from Lois. She is, it should be said, convinced of the importance of being creative and wishes to stimulate this quality in her daughter, projecting in this way onto her daughter some of her own ambitions of being a writer. Lois herself has always wanted to emulate her older brother's and sister's intellectual achievements and has pretty well internalized most of her mother's standards. There is thus no evident conflict in family relations.

The Blacks, on the other hand, are an example of a family of divergers: two of their children were amongst the high creatives of the Getzels and Jackson study. The most striking thing about their apartment is the mass of books and magazines that litter the rooms and fill every nook and cranny.

Father is a biologist, mother edited a small newspaper

until the birth of her first child. Mrs Black is at ease with the world and herself, relaxed and frank about the family. According to her, family life centres on father who dominates it and whom the children follow. The mother believes in guarding the children's health, but otherwise giving them their freedom, out of respect for their individuality. She talks to John about school, but does not want to pry. Mrs Black is pleased that her children are different from her as a child in that they are more secure and independent. There is open disagreement between John and his father on choice of a career (John wants to go in for the arts, in particular music, his father wants him to be a scientist). However, in spite of this disagreement, the essence of the father-son relationship is based on shared interests—they watch fights on TV together and 'egghead programmes' on Sunday afternoons and join up in other activities.

John's mother stresses the closeness of the family ties—how they go on holiday together and do things together—something that irks the children a little. The family is marked by both close and strong bonds of attachment and by currents of disagreement, especially with father.

These are but case histories and should not be taken as typical of the characteristics of *all* divergers' (and convergers') families. Several investigators, some of whom we have already met in previous chapters, have, however, looked into the question of home background. A number of studies (e.g. MacKinnon, 1962, Schaefer and Anastasi, 1968) have found that creative individuals tend to have fathers or other relatives who provide for them models of effectiveness and resourcefulness and people within their environment who share their field of interests.

What is very noticeable is that the parents of creative children show unusual respect for them as individuals and have great confidence in their ability to do 'the right thing'. They thus grant them considerable autonomy to explore their world and encourage them in independent, mature activities. The parents, in other words, show a high level of tolerance and a low level of control (cf. MacKinnon, 1962, Drevdahl, 1964, Nichols and Holland, 1963). No doubt, their parents' willingness to place confidence in their ability to conduct themselves reasonably contributed very largely to the later autonomy and independent-mindedness of these creative persons.

Weisberg and Springer (1961) did a detailed study of the families of thirty-two highly gifted nine-year-olds, selected from a population of 7,000, who were given criterion tests of divergent thinking. The parents of high divergers showed expressiveness (i.e. openness in human contact) together with a lack of domination of their children. They also accepted any regressive tendencies their children might show, i.e. they were tolerant of a temporary return to baby-ish behaviour without demanding mature attitudes all the time. The association between these parent variables and divergent ability was highly significant. It was also found —though at a slightly lower level of significance—that divergers tended to have mothers who displayed very little trace of compulsive behaviour and that the fathers had a closer relationship with their children than did fathers of non-divergers. Other results, though suggestive, lacked statistical significance, e.g. that there was a tendency for parents of divergers to demand less conformity to parental values and for religion to be a less powerful force in these homes (a finding duplicated by MacKinnon), or a tendency for parents to be strong individualistic personalities not averse to voicing their feelings openly.

When we speak of children's independence and autonomy in these families, we should not, however, equate this with complete permissiveness and an absence of discipline. MacKinnon (1962) mentions consistent and predictable discipline and Mrs Black, quoted above, indicated spankings. There is also another, more painful, side to the parents' non-involvement in their children's private lives and the granting of autonomy. Often this meant that one or both parents were somewhat distant and aloof, and this may not be unconnected with the often observed fact that divergent children engage in more solitary activities than do others (MacKinnon, 1962, Stein, 1963b, Drevdahl, 1964). In the same vein another study (Helson, 1966) noted that women who scored highly on tests of imagination and artisticness had mothers who were less nurturant and ambitious than the mothers of low scorers. We must not imagine, therefore, that creative persons were blessed with childhood days of uninterrupted sunshine and ideal happiness.

If we look at the social class the divergers' families belonged to, we find that they were all middle or upper-middle class. MacKinnon (1962) noted that there was no financial hardship present in the home; Weisberg and Springer (1961) found that the degree to which father was professionally autonomous was very significantly associated with children's divergent ability. It will be recalled from the last chapter that Getzels and Jackson's convergers on the whole had parents who were professionals and university trained ('bureaucrats'), whilst divergers predominantly had fathers who were in business ('entrepreneurs'). Although by no means all researches have confirmed such a finding, Weisberg and Springer's observation that degree of autonomy of the father is related to the children's divergent ability points in the same direction. A family which is not enmeshed in hierarchical subordination and not accustomed and tied to following the rules of a bureaucratic machine may be able to create a climate in which risk-taking is seen as part of the routine of life, and is encouraged and autonomy becomes meaningful for both parents and children.

MacKinnon (1962) noted that the families of the more creative architects tended to move their place of abode more frequently. Whilst this meant an enrichment of experience and stimulation for the children, it also meant that the families often found themselves uprooted and implanted in an unfamiliar neighbourhood with which they were not socially integrated. This fact may also have been a contributory cause of the feeling of isolation and aloneness and the solitary activities often reported by creative men. A final demographic finding, repeatedly observed, e.g. by Roe (1952), is that eminent men are first-born children more than chance would allow.

To sum up, what is an overall picture of families of those who have creative, or at least divergent, gifts? They would seem to be middle-class with father having considerable autonomy in his profession or business. The father thus provides a model of autonomy, as well as of general effectiveness and the parents, in turn, grant similar autonomy to their children. The mother will also often have had a career in her own right before marriage. The parents exhibit enthusiasm for creative activities, encourage their children's curiosity and exploratory urge and stimulate them to independent achievement. However, this is done without pressure for high standards or particular accomplishments, since autonomy here means that the parents do not intrude, but allow their children to develop at their own pace and in their own desired direction, even to the point of being tolerant of some backsliding to more infantile behaviour. The children's autonomy may also be bought at the expense of some closeness and warmth in family relations. Nor is the family necessarily an entirely harmonious one: open expressions of feelings and sometimes of disagreement will be a normal part of family life.

The following is a vivid illustration, written by an ordinary housewife, of what actually goes on in such a household (Thorne, 1967):

Neither Perfect Housekeeping nor House Beautiful dominates our home. We live in a university town in a high, square, old-fashioned house. The upstairs bathroom contains an immense closet with wide shelves for quilts and blankets, but we don't keep our extra bedding there. Instead we keep stacks of National Geographics, all the art work and notebooks which our five children have lugged home from school and wanted saved, lots of maps, and a stack of very large envelopes containing pictures and clippings about American history, English history, Renaissance art, religion, plants, animals, etc.

A child comes home from school and says, 'We're studying Abraham Lincoln. What've we got?' So we retire to the bathroom to emerge presently with one magazine article, several pictures, and a yellowed replica of the newspaper telling of Lincoln's assassination, this latter a souvenir saved from a trip to Washington, D.C. The shelves also hold scrapbooks on art, space, elementary French, a year spent in Tennessee, a collection of bookmarks, etc.

Precariously stacked on the very top shelf are rolled-up homemade charts, mostly on shelf paper. One chart shows the relative size of the planets. Another lists famous persons of history, arranged by civilization and chronology. Another is a rough drawing of the world with small pictures of fruits, vegetables, and flowers pasted onto the area of origin. There is also a chart showing routes our great-great-parents took from Europe to America and on across to the far West. These and others have each at some time been pinned to the dining room or kitchen wallpaper. We live with pin-pricked wallpaper, just as we live with shredded upholstery where the cat sharpens her claws.

By the way of further inventory let us consider the kitchen cupboards. The glassed-in shelves intended for lovely china and glassware are filled instead with games, puzzles, stamp collections, two decorated cans which contain embroidery floss and half-completed dishtowels, two sets of knitting progress—I think they are to be bedroom slippers. My silverware box does not contain silverware; it has been subdivided for a shell collection which has overflowed into Christmas card boxes. There are tennis and badminton rackets and three cameras.

Scattered in various other places are scratch paper, type paper, pencils, crayons, scissors, water colours in small jars, three kinds of glue, chalk, compass, rulers, three kinds of tape, balls of string, and ink. At this very moment two children are at the kitchen table writing with a pheasant feather and ink, just to see how it might have felt to be a scribe in colonial days.

My theory is this: helping children to love learning involves first, creative materials. I have named some, but the last thing on earth that we ever call them is creative materials. They are 'stuff'.

Second: Love of learning requires enthusiasm. If parents are enthusiastic their offspring will pick it up by contagion. In fact the offspring will spring off in directions where their parents can only stumble, music, in our case. Four-dimensional geometry was its climax.

When our oldest son was about four years old, he brought into the kitchen a brown paper sack of clods. He had seen his father collect soil samples in brown paper sacks, so he had invaded a vacant lot and gathered his own sample. Then he asked me to get out our food chopper, an affair of cast metal, and he began to grind up the clods. It was hard work but he stayed with it to the end. Our kitchen looked like the Oklahoma dust bowl and the blade of my chopper was ruined forever.

However, a family can only work within the limits of the culture in which it finds itself, and the individual will be profoundly influenced by his contacts with others and by the subtle influence of the broader environment, no less than by his family. In how far does a culture tolerate deviations from the traditional, in how far does it allow the individual opportunities for creative experiences? Does it hold to values which stress conformity to established norms? All this will have a bearing on the flowering of creative production within that society. As Stein (1963a) writes:

the extent to which a variety of creative products are developed depends on the extent to which cultural influences permit the development of both freedom between the individual and his environment and freedom within the individual; on the extent to which the culture encourages diversity and tolerates the seeming ambiguity that such diversity suggests.

Torrance (1965) investigated the views of teachers in five different cultures—the U.S.A., Germany, India, Greece and the Philippines—on creativity-connected behaviour and found that teachers in all cultures to varying degrees disapproved of such behaviour as asking questions, guessing, being independent in judgment and thinking, being intuitive, being willing to take risks, being unwilling to accept an opinion on mere authority and, on the other hand, to varying degrees approved of the virtues of obedience and courtesy and the like. It should be noted that not all teachers disapproved (or approved) of the appropriate kind of behaviour. Disapproval and approval was rather a relative thing and amongst these nations the U.S.A. was relatively closest to the creative 'ideal', the Philippines furthest away. It is not too far-fetched to suggest that creative production and innovations in societies will be related to attitudes such as these.

Vernon (1967a) carried out a study with divergent tests amongst English, Hebridean, Eskimo and (Canadian) Indian children. The Hebridean children generally resembled the English with a certain amount of restriction of creative imagination. In reading the following about Eskimos and Indians it will be remembered (cf. chapter 2) that 'ideational fluency' is a measure of the quality of material produced, whereas 'originality' is a factor indicating the cleverness or uniqueness of ideas.

Both Eskimos and Indians, though coming from very poor economic and cultural backgrounds and being retarded in English, were often as high in ideational fluency as the English reference group, or higher, though the

75

quality of their associations or stories was poorer. The Indians in particular showed strong perseveration and lack of originality which can probably be attributed to their lack of cultural stimulation, extreme conservatism and non-cooperation with the white civilization.

Eskimos, however, obtained scores on several originality variables comparable to those of the British samples. This fits in with their greater adaptability and initiative relative to the Indian groups. (Vernon, 1967a)

Here, too, then we see the influence of cultural traditions and attitudes.

What explanatory theory will account for the relationships obtained? One such theory that integrates the various aspects of developmental influences on creativity has been proposed by Harvey (1966). He starts with the proposition that all natural systems and organisms evolve by means of the processes of differentiation and integration in which initially undifferentiated parts of the system become progressively more specific and adapted to their purpose, at the same time becoming interrelated to each other as parts of a higher-order system. The processes of differentiation and integration give rise to differing levels of organization in the systems which can be ordered along the dimension of *concreteness–abstractness*. Harvey isolated four levels along this dimension, each of which characterizes the way a system (person) may function. The first level represents the most concrete mode of construing and responding to the world and is assumed to evolve from a training history in which the developing individual has been restricted in exploration of his environment. The fourth level, at the more abstract end of the continuum, is seen as the consequence of childhood freedom to explore both the social and physical aspects of one's environment, to solve problems and evolve solutions without fear of punishment for deviating from established truth. On theoretical grounds and on the basis of empirical investigation it can be said that a person at the more abstract level is likely to engage in a greater amount of exploration and to produce more novel and flexible solutions to problems than a person at the opposite end, in short, he will be more creative.

A certain amount of corroboration for the connection between these types of developmental history and level of abstraction has been found in an investigation by Cross (1966). A parallel theory regarding rigidity—flexibility has been put forward by Thompson (1966), this time based on animal studies. He suggests that at a developmental stage when emotional responses are being crystallized, strong conditioning to the 'familiar' may lower the probability that alternative responses will produce reward, with the result that fewer new responses will be emitted and the organism will be afraid to see new things or try new modes of action. During a later stage when instrumental responses, which enable the individual to cope with the outside world, are being evolved, severe restriction of practice in perceptual and motor activity may tend to favour rigid behaviour simply by limiting the range of stimulus complexity and response repertory.

Pre-school education

How can we compensate for a home background that lacks the climate and the kind of stimulation conducive to creative endeavour? We know we have to start early, in the pre-school years, when the child's mind is most sensitive to changes in stimulation. Hence the importance that has been attached to pre-school education for disadvantaged children, especially in the United States. The 'progressive' nursery school has ever since the thirties sought to surround the child with stimuli that were to facilitate the development of his sense perception, of his cognitive structures and of his social interaction, though it did this in a diffuse way, deliberately eschewing 'training'. It stimulated the child to 'experiment' with sand and water, to explore shapes by means of modelling clay, wire, etc., and to imitate and prepare himself for the adult world with the help of shop or street fittings etc. It encouraged the expression of feelings, impulses and fantasies not only through dramatization, but also through the media of paint, finger paint or clay. Many of these activities, particularly dramatization, painting or modelling, automatically give the child the opportunity to create something for which no blueprint has been laid down, in other words, to be 'creative'.

The general rationale for such a programme is based on the notion that enrichment of environmental stimulation will lead to greater intellectual competence—that is, thinking abilities all round will be more effective, not only divergent abilities. So-called 'cognitive psychologists', such as Hunt (1961) or Bruner (1960), laid great emphasis on early cognitive development and the optimal stimulation that will facilitate it. These concepts came to be applied particularly to the education of culturally deprived children, since it was thought that their handicaps, and consequent low school attainments, arose, to a large extent at least, from lack of normal stimulation in their homes. (They did not usually attend nursery schools which tended to be the playgrounds of the middle classes.)

Although the tendency in 'progressive' nursery schools was to inculcate skills in 'how to get along with people' and to stress social and emotional development (and, as we saw, the opportunity for creative work automatically went along with this), they did not by any means neglect cognitive skills. The cognitive trend in the fifties and sixties, however, shifted the emphasis towards greater attention to language and conceptual attainments. The question is how much directed training in specific verbal and cognitive skills is optimal for the child's intellectual development. Amongst the various programmes for disadvantaged pre-school children (and this includes five-year-olds in the United States) which were started in the sixties, the 'Head Start' classes were probably nearest in conception and practice to what might paradoxically be called the 'traditional progressive' nursery school. Head Start classes, too, included cognitive activities in their programme, though in a less structured and directed way than some of the other programmes to be discussed later; for instance, the teacher might read from an 'activity' book which required the child to identify pictures on the page and then pat the bunny or feel the beard, or the children would sing songs which required actions to be matched to the words or number songs, such as 'One-two, buckle my shoe'. With a frequently very good teacher-pupil ratio went considerable individual attention and while the classes developed social skills they placed considerable emphasis on language development, but in a non-drill way.

One step further in systematic cognitive training was taken by intervention programmes for disadvantaged pre-schoolers, such as those developed by the Institute for Developmental Studies in New York or by George Peabody College in Tennessee. These programmes employ conventional nursery equipment, but in a more deliberate manner, using, for instance, wooden cubes or a language lotto to teach vocabulary, number, colour and prepositions such as 'on', 'under', etc. In a sense they are reformed nursery schools.

A completely different approach to cognitive development in the pre-school years is represented by the 'Responsive Environment', a method evolved by O. K. Moore (1966). The method hinges on the 'Talking Typewriter'. This system in its fully automated form, called 'E.R.E.' (Edison Responsive Environment), involves an electric typewriter, a display screen on which letters, words or sentences can be exhibited together with accompanying pictures, a slide projector, a microphone and a speaker—

all connected to a small computer and costing $40,000. The method consists in letting the child teach himself skills through his own guided discoveries without overt adult interference. A picture and the word 'c a t' would, for instance, appear on the screen and the child be asked to type the word. All keys, except 'c', are locked until the child has successfully depressed this key, when the machine types and the speaker pronounces 'c'. Then the key for 'a' is unlocked by the E.R.E., and so forth. At a later stage the child will indicate his thoughts or a story into a dictating machine and then type this material via the E.R.E., and thus reading and writing will be intimately connected with his own personal ideas. Whether the child works at the machine or not is left to his own choice, but the children, loving gadgets as they do, are all said to work most of the time and three- to four-year-old (mainly bright children have learned to write their own stories and to read children's books this way.

The most extreme method in structuring and directing children's learning is the 'pressure-cooker' approach or the 'grind-and-drill' method with which the names of Bereiter and Engelmann (1966) are associated. Although it is hailed as an innovation in America, it is in reality a combination of the drill method, widespread in nineteenth-century British schools, with the screaming enthusiasm of a revivalist meeting. The teacher holds up a picture of a rifle and says. 'This is a ——.' Child: 'Gun'. Teacher: 'Good. It is a gun. Let's all say it. This is a gun. This is a gun. This is a gun.' And the drill proceeds in lockstep fashion with various attention-holding devices, such as deliberate misstatements by the teacher. Nothing here is left to the children, the teacher dictates everything. The method can be applied to vocabulary, letters, arithmetic and one of its endearing— and seemingly effective—features is the enthusiastic roaring of teacher and children alike.

What of creativity? Some of the intervention programmes for disadvantaged pre-schoolers described above encourage exploratory and creative activities and some of the most successful methods of teaching reading to young children, e.g. Montessori's or Moore's, enlist the child's creativity by letting him write his own words or stories almost from the beginning. However, the 'pressure-cooker' approach has very little time for this. The authors consider that divergent-thinking tasks must take lower priority than the mastery of skills fundamental to convergent thinking, but they do include some divergent tasks in their programme, e.g. inventing new verses for songs, or generating explanations for events in stories.

The project is, of course, designed for children whose cognitive development has been severely handicapped from the start by an impoverished and constricting home environment. It may be that the best we can do for them is to train them in very specific skills to enable them to take advantage of the normal school in order to acquire the basic three Rs, the bread and butter of life. Perhaps the jam—creative achievements—is not for them. Yet we are left with some unease that this project goes so directly counter to all we know about nurturing creative talent. It ignores, for instance, Thompson's conclusion (see previous section), backed by some evidence, that at a certain stage strong conditioning to the familiar may lead to the result that the organism will be afraid to see new things or try new modes of action and that at a later stage severe restriction of practice in perceptual and motor activity may favour rigid behaviour. It also takes no account of the huge body of work amassed by Piaget which led him to the conclusion which essentially boils down to this: if we want a child truly to acquire a new concept and reach a higher conceptual stage we must put him in the way of discovering it for himself, with us providing the props, guides and wherewithal. The teacher, in other words, is there to create the problem situation, ask the appropriate question and offer conflicting evidence if the child is too easily satisfied with his own less mature solutions.

Since the Bereiter and Engelmann project is specifically geared to children from the lowest social classes, whereas middle-class children attend 'progressive' nursery schools with their creative activities, it seems to me the programme harks back to nineteenth-century attitudes in that it creates two contrasting educational approaches, one for the élite and another one for the masses, the latter consisting of a little reading, writing and arithmetic, enough to fit the children for the station in life to which God has called them. Is it a system designed to produce conforming automata? Pines (1966) asks: 'Have (these children) learned, deep down, to parrot unquestioningly whatever they are told by people in authority?'

As for fostering curiosity, exploratory impulses and creativity, we are really no further than Susan Isaacs was in the Malting House School in the twenties.

Developing productive thinking

In the eighteenth century the German poet Schiller wrote to a friend who complained to him of his lack of creative powers:

> Apparently it is not good—and indeed it hinders the creative work of the mind—if the intellect examines too closely the ideas already pouring in, as it were, at the gates ... In the case of a creative mind, it seems to me, the intellect has withdrawn its watchers from the gates, and the ideas rush in pell-mell, and only then does it review and inspect the multitude. You worthy critics, or whatever you call yourselves, are ashamed or afraid of the momentary and passing madness which is found in all real creators, the longer or shorter duration of which distinguishes the thinking artist from the dreamer. Hence your complaints of unfruitfulness, for you reject too soon and discriminate too severely. (Freud, 1938)

Schiller here—long before Freud—clearly recognized the importance of the unconscious as a source of creative ideas as well as the importance of deferring critical judgment on them at the vital moments of creation. Osborn (1953) was the first to apply this principle of 'separating the process of producing ideas from the process of evaluating them'—to stimulate creativity systematically in a commercial setting, in fact an advertising agency, and he gave it the name of 'brainstorming'. Typically it involves gathering a few people together in a group and instructing them to pour out any idea that occurs to them on a certain subject, however trivial, silly or far-fetched it may seem, without attempting to assess its value. Parnes (1963) has applied the technique to students and has built regular college courses at Buffalo, New York, around it. Moreover, he has been at pains to dispel the misconception that the principle of deferred judgment is applicable to group production only, since he used it with individuals working on their own.

In the course at Buffalo students are taught the concepts of Osborn's book *Applied Imagination* (1953). Various kinds of blocks to creative thinking are demonstrated and discussed: perceptual blocks, e.g. too narrow a focus, difficulty in isolating problems; cultural and emotional blocks, e.g. effects of conformity, excessive faith in reason or logic, reliance on authority and fear of mistakes. Students are taught the principle of deferred judgment which, in Parnes' words (1963), means: 'during the effort to generate ideas, the judicial process is deliberately suspended; evaluation is deferred in order to allow full play to imagination.' Students are given practice in attribute listing, e.g. in thinking up a variety of uses for a piece of paper; students are taught to look at each attribute of the paper, its whiteness, its four corners, its straight edges, etc., each of which may suggest a number of possible uses. When considering a problem they are encouraged to make up as long a list of questions as possible about the problem ('idea-spurring questions') and to write down as many facts as they can think of. Only at a later stage will they pick out the most relevant questions and the most important facts. Three points are stressed:

> The importance of taking notes (keeping a record of ideas that come to one at any and all times, rather than only while one is working on a problem), the value of setting deadlines and quotas for production of ideas and the advantage of setting aside certain times and places for deliberate idea production. (Parnes, 1963)

To test the efficacy of the deferred-judgment principle students were asked to think up tentative solutions to assigned problems, at first applying evaluation while they were doing this and then deliberately postponing evaluation. Under the first condition they produced an average of 2.5 good ideas, under the latter condition 4.3 good ideas, the quality of the ideas being assessed by judges. This finding, we should note, has not been left uncontradicted in the literature. Torrance (1963) found that when elementary school children were told simply to produce as many ideas as possible they generated *fewer* responses than when they were instructed to put down as many good and original ideas as possible. An interesting comparison between the output of groups of four people working as groups and others working individually, but subsequently allotted to 'nominal' groups, was carried out by Taylor *et al.* (1958). The outcome showed individual effort to be superior, but both sets of subjects used the deferred-judgment principle so that the advantage of the essence of 'brainstorming' is left unchallenged by this result.

Parnes also showed that his training had generalized effects: when he matched students trained in his technique with untrained students both the quantity and the quality of ideas produced by trained students in response to divergent tests were superior and, moreover, the trained students gained significantly in 'dominance', as measured by a personality test.

Interesting possibilities open up if the principles of brainstorming and creative thinking can be integrated in conventional subject courses. Economics, marketing and physics are subjects in which college courses have been modified in this way. Workshops have also been held where teachers of diverse subjects devised ways of integrating creative methodologies in their respective subject-matter fields.

A more sophisticated and somewhat more deep-searching approach to increasing creative production has been evolved under the name of 'Synectics' (Gordon, 1961). 'Synectics', from the Greek, means literally, 'joining together of diverse elements' and stresses the same process that in chapter 1 was described as 'fusion of two matrices' (Koestler's terminology). Synectics also, like brainstorming, encourages the spontaneous and free flow of ideas without the intervention of criticism, and the technique involves working in groups. However, the methodology has gone further in devising conscious mechanisms intended to facilitate the process of unconscious fermentation. It makes use of two basic mechanisms: 'making-the-strange-familiar', and 'making-the-familiar-strange'. The first means familiarizing oneself with the problem and analysing its parts, the second is a less-known procedure, peculiar to synectics, and involves looking at what is old and familiar from fresh points of view, to regain a certain innocence of vision. The process consists of deliberately seeking out different analogies, three distinct types having been defined: the Personal, Direct and Symbolic Analogy. Personal analogy is imagining one's feelings if one were, say, the shoe box for which various uses are sought. Direct analogy can be illustrated by Graham Bell seeing the similarity between the membrane of the ear and an artificial membrane that would make the telephone possible. The most fertile source of direct analogies proved to be biology, in particular sexual anatomy. Symbolic analogy consists of restating in verbal-symbolic form the meaning of key-words, e.g. 'target' can be re-interpreted as 'focused desire'.

Special training procedures have also been introduced in schools, the best known project being that of Crutchfield and Covington which attempts to enhance efficient prob-lem-solving skills in ten-eleven-year-old children (Covington *et al.*, 1969, Crutchfield, 1965, Olton and Crutchfield, 1969). The method consists of a self-instructional programme con-tained in sixteen booklets. The authors are themselves aware of the paradox inherent in attempting to increase creative powers by means of programmed instruction. Does a programme with its rigidly established steps, which are the same for everybody, not produce a uniformity of thought which is detrimental to the very quality of crea-tiveness which the authors seek to foster? Furthermore, how can a diversity of ideas be stimulated in programmed instruction which in its normal form depends on reinforc-ing only the *one* correct response? The authors think they have overcome some of these disadvantages by using a more flexible form of programming; indeed, a variety of responses is asked for at the various stages. They have been able to deal with the problem that a programme can allow only one correct solution, if it is to reinforce without human intervention, by concentrating their efforts in the area of solving detective problems or mysteries where, in-deed, after a variety of initial response possibilities there is only one 'correct' answer.

The booklets have a continuous story-line which follows the adventures of Jim and Lila, two school-children, as they try to solve a series of detective and other mysteries, helped by their wise and friendly Uncle John. The method, above all, gives instruction in various strategies helpful in problem-solving and many of these are very similar to those taught in the brainstorming and synectics techniques.

Uncle John notices Jim's silence:

FIG. 4

Now, what will happen as Jim and Lila take Uncle John's advice? Turn the page to find out.

FIG. 5

FIG. 6

89

You try making a list, too. Go back to pages 8 and 9 and read the story again. Then pick out each of the main things in the story and write it down:

_____

_____

_____

_____

_____

_____

FIG. 7

Thus the programme points out such techniques as formulating the problem, asking relevant questions, the generation of many ideas, the search for uncommon ideas, the transformation of the problem in new ways, sensitivity to odd and discrepant fact and openness to metaphorical and analogical hints leading to solutions. The problems are so arranged that the alert child can find the solution one step ahead of the booklet, so that he is given a sense of discovery and success. (A part of the programme is reproduced on pp. 87-90).

In experimenting with the programme Crutchfield and Covington found that training resulted in markedly improved problem-solving performance. Moreover the beneficial effects generalized to other divergent-thinking tasks and, the problem-solving skills, at least, seemed to be firmly established and persisted over some time.

These are but beginnings and much more work will have to be done, especially since the results are not completely free from doubts and contradictions. However, the prospects seem to be bright for increasing effectiveness in problem-solving by teaching what are essentially deliberate strategies of flexibility and variability of response. Problem-solving depends on a synthesis of secondary-process and primary-process thinking (for an explanation of these terms see chapter 3) and what we are facilitating is the secondary-process part, how to adopt rational strategies. Whether primary-process thinking can be taught similarly is a moot point.

91

5

The creative child at school

Is education biased against creativity?

In almost all statements in recent years by professors of education, writers, scientists and other public figures about the need for change and flexibility in education, there has been contained some diatribe against the iniquities of the school system that demands conformity and parroting rather than thinking, and against the teachers who are hidebound in their time-worn attitudes and neither recognize nor wish to recognize the creativity in front of their eyes. Yet what could be more creative than helping children to grow in maturity, to acquire skills of brain as well as of hand, to become familiar with and make their own some of the accomplishments of civilization? Potentially, at least, the teacher is a creator and his material is the minds of children.

It may be that we can criticize schools—and universities and colleges—for the lack of academic rewards in terms of grades and acknowledgment that creative achievement receives. It may also be true that a disproportionately large number of creatively gifted individuals 'drop out' of school and college, as has been shown for America. In making such criticisms, however, we must bear in mind that schools are *institutions* dedicated to the transmission of culture and social norms and to the development of the individual within this culture and its rationality. Institutions are built on common pursuit of rational goals, by their very nature are somewhat slow to change and able to tolerate only a certain amount of deviation from the rules thought necessary for the achievement of the common purpose. In this sense institutions and creative individuals are natural opposites. It is hardly surprising that we often find divergers dissatisfied, because they are at odds with the rationality of the institution and diverge from its aims. They not only want to 'do their own thing', but also be free not to do anything, not only to drop out of the 'rat race', but also out of their own growth, out of active life altogether. A year or more out of school or college may indeed be the proper response to their needs at the time and serve their eventual growth and maturation, as in this instance:

At age 20, I left college because it had come to be, for me, death-dealing. I was growing weak and scrawny because I could not get from living there what my life needed for its growing. I was ill-fitted to the setting as I saw it. In nine months out, much of my time was spent in the lap of nature, communicating with that primal structure. This offered ground for giving form to scientific questions. I returned to college, resolved to see, beneath the operation, what was giving life and what was giving death to those within it. With the help of a vital teacher, I found my way to make college life rewarding ... (Mooney, 1967)

In other words, it is the creative individual who is ill-adapted to the institution, not the institution which is ill-fitted to the requirements of the majority whom it serves. Nor should we forget that the school may serve a useful purpose if it provides a symbol of authority to kick against. The diverger can rebel against the triviality and authority-ridden nature of the school and feel good about it. If the school was entirely tailored to his wishes, what would be left to rebel against?

Teachers' and pupils' attitudes

Getzels and Jackson (1962) asked teachers to rate their pupils on the degree to which they enjoyed having them in class. The outcome was that the high IQ students were rated as more liked than the average students, but the high creatives were rated only at average level, and this in spite of the fact that their school performance was on a par with that of the high IQ students and rather better than their own IQ level would lead one to predict. Torrance (1962) reports very similar findings. Hasan and Butcher (1966) replicated the Getzels and Jackson study in Scotland and also found that teachers rated the likeability of pupils in the 'high creative' group—in contrast to those who combined high creativity with high IQ—only at average level. Divergent pupils may, of course, be awkward to have in a class. Their very independence of mind and differing values may lead them to be obstructionist and perhaps we ought to realize that obstructiveness and cussedness can be part of a creative streak. There is the unexpected way of looking at things, leading to the seemingly impudent question at the wrong time. Cropley (1967) recounts an incident in a Canadian elementary school when the class had been set the task of drawing a head to give the teacher some time for her paper work. Up comes a child, who had been troublesome before, and asks whether he should draw the outside or the inside of the head! Not surprisingly, the teacher, more than busy at the time, exploded.

Moreover, creative children may see possibilities in a problem or an experiment that the teacher missed when he prepared the lesson and which therefore may disconcert him. All this would lead to difficulties in the class, though the more experienced, self-assured and less rigid teacher will usually be able to take them in his stride. Nevertheless, many teachers will have a less favourable attitude to creative (and obstructive?) children than to the more conforming types.

Divergent children may thus find themselves in an anti-teacher position, a situation which the older ones, at any rate, may, however, enjoy. What of their popularity with their peers? Torrance (1967b) noted that divergent boys in the first three years at school tended to be labelled by other children as having 'silly' or 'crazy' ideas by their peers, whereas creative girls did not gain such a reputation. The danger is that under such social pressure divergent boys will, by the time they are nine or ten, have learned to be evasive and to keep their thoughts to themselves with a consequent loss of that precious spark of originality. However, as was pointed out in chapter 3, we have found in English primary schools (Haddon and Lytton, 1968) that popularity goes with creative abilities in schools that value informal methods and creative learning, and goes with IQ in schools that favour more formal approaches. At the secondary level, too, we found, popularity is associated with IQ in grammar schools, but with creative abilities in some secondary modern schools, relationships that will reflect the value systems of the different schools.

In looking at these somewhat contradictory results we must note that several years elapsed between the Torrance investigations (about 1959) and ours in England (1965), years which saw an enormous expansion of interest in creative behaviour and ways of fostering it, as well as a popularization of these concepts. I suspect that the climate in schools overall has been changing in favour of divergent thinking—partly due to the efforts of creativity enthusiasts such as Getzels, Jackson and Torrance—and that as a result divergent children find themselves nowadays socially at much less of a disadvantage.

Achievements

As we have noted in the last section, Getzels and Jackson showed that high divergent abilities were as indicative of high scholastic performance as was high IQ in the high schools that they studied. Wallach and Wing (1969) similarly found that high divergers and convergers were both equally superior in academic performance to the population from which they were drawn, although divergent and convergent abilities seemed to overlap very little (i.e. had low correlations with each other). Hasan and Butcher (1966) also confirmed in their Scottish study that the aggregate creativity score predicted attainment in English and arithmetic almost as well as did the VRQ (i.e. IQ) score. However, their 'high creativity' group, constituted, in the Getzels and Jackson manner, by those who were in the top 20 per cent for divergent tests, but not in the top 20 per cent for IQ, had significantly lower attainment scores than the 'high intelligence' group, although the 'high creatives' performance was somewhat above the average of the total sample. It is interesting to note that their 'high creativity *and* high intelligence' group scored highest of all in English and had attainments in arithmetic that were not significantly lower than those of the 'high intelligence' group. We may assume, without being accused of wild speculation, that it is from this group that the men and women who will make the greatest creative contribution to society are most likely to be drawn; hence special interest attached to their characteristics at school, and conversely the fact that Getzels and Jackson deliberately excluded such a group from their research seriously detracts from its value.

There is another way of looking at the relationship between divergent ability and school achievements. The way that children acquire knowledge and skills may, after all, affect their final attainments. Indeed, Torrance (1967a) quotes a number of studies, ranging from 1934 to 1963, that indicate that when knowledge is obtained by authority-centred teaching (i.e. receptive, directed learning) traditional measures of intelligence or scholastic aptitude are the best predictors, whereas if knowledge is obtained in more creative ways, e.g. by 'discovery' learning, tests of fluency, originality, etc., seem to predict attainments better than does IQ. Torrance draws an important educational conclusion from this:

> Children learn best when given opportunities to learn in ways best suited to their motivations and abilities. Whenever teachers change their ways of teaching in significant ways, a different group of learners become the stars or high achievers.... Somewhere, however, we need to re-assess our objectives and determine what criteria we should be interested in predicting. This would probably lead to a recognition that we need multiple criteria and that we should value a variety of different kinds of achievement. (Torrance, 1967a)

A fact that is of interest in this connection and that affords a fascinating glimpse into the teaching and criteria of arithmetic is the following: a study by Yamamoto (1963) showed that the combination of *low* teacher creativity and *low* pupil creativity resulted in the *highest* achievement in arithmetic, while the combination of *low* teacher creativity and *high* pupil creativity yielded the worst results!

A propitious school climate

Though it is doubtful whether the genius of a Shakespeare, a Michelangelo or an Einstein is ever created at school, at somewhat lower levels it is likely that the school can play a part in increasing or decreasing divergent abilities and divergent attitudes in the children it has in its care for five hours a day. All of us have something of the spark of originality that education can blow upon and make brighter.

There are two main ways in which a school may hope to enhance children's creative abilities. One is to introduce special educational experiences for deliberately training creative thinking or problem-solving skills as such, unrelated to normal school subjects, and these techniques, e.g. brainstorming, synectics and the 'Productive Thinking Program' we discussed in the last chapter. The other way is to generate a 'creative spirit' in the school and to adopt an experimental, creative, open-ended approach to learning in each individual field of the ordinary curriculum. What matters here is the way language, mathematics, science, etc., are taught and the attitudes teachers adopt towards the process of education. This is the topic with which we are concerned now.

Since the school is only one factor in the development of a child's abilities, the preponderant influence being the home, it is likely that measurable differences between school and school will be small. Nevertheless, a colleague and I set out to see whether the effects that the differing climates of an 'informal' and a 'formal' primary school may have on the divergent abilities of the children can be detected (Haddon and Lytton, 1968). The two types of school which were contrasted were the formal, or traditional, school which places emphasis on convergent thinking and authoritative learning and the informal, or progressive, school, where the emphasis is on self-initiated learning and creative activities. The criteria used for distinguishing between the two types were mainly: emphasis on achievement, rigidity of time-table, predominance of class lessons and control of movement within the school. Two pairs of contrasted primary schools matched for socio-economic background were chosen after consultation with lecturers from a college of education who were familiar with the area and on advice from a local inspector of schools. One of each type was situated in a predominantly middle-class urban area, the other school in each category drew children from a more mixed social background in a different urban area. The mean VRQ of the formal schools combined was 101·75 and that of the informal schools 101·14, so that the contrasting groups were equated for verbal reasoning ability. 211 eleven- to twelve-year-old children, covering the whole ability range, were given the tests in their last term at school. The divergent tests used were three non-verbal and three verbal tests, partly taken over or adapted from Torrance's tests (Torrance, 1962), partly devised (see Appendix). A sociometric survey was also included.

The results bore out the prediction that children from informal schools, which can be assumed to encourage the growth of attitudes to learning associated with divergency, would have higher divergent scores than children from formal schools. On five out of the six tests the means of the informal schools were significantly higher and on the sixth test the difference, though it did not reach statistical significance, was in the predicted direction. If the experiment thus showed informal schools to have a beneficial effect on the development of creative abilities, I should stress that the study did not compare good *versus* bad schools, but good schools of two types, which operate with a somewhat different emphasis. It was not permissiveness which was the distinguishing criterion of informality as opposed to formality. The most striking difference lay in the degree of emphasis placed upon self-initiated learning. One may speculate that behind this emphasis in the informal schools, and fundamental to its success, lay the pattern of interpersonal relationships within the school. One's impression in the informal school was of a relaxed, friendly atmosphere in which children moved freely, both within the classroom and in the school generally. Particularly noticeable was the freedom of access to the libraries and the extent to which children worked in them without supervision. The formal schools were not unfriendly, but one sensed a tighter rein and a firmer directive and classwork was more in evidence.

Moreover, the effect of spending the formative early school years in a school atmosphere conducive to open-ended learning seems to persist. We followed up the sample four years later (Haddon and Lytton, 1971) when the children were fifteen and some of them were just about to leave school for the adult world. The children from both formal and informal schools were intermingled across a variety of schools—secondary modern, comprehensive, grammar—and we found it impossible to assess the climate of these schools for formality or informality because of the within-school variation from department to department. The same divergent tests were administered again and, in spite of the differing school experiences of the intervening four years, the effect of the type of primary school the children had attended was still clearly and significantly noticeable, children from informal primary schools out-performing those from formal primary schools. On the other hand, allowance being made for the pervasive VRQ effect, the official category of secondary school that the children attended—secondary modern, comprehensive, or grammar—did not seem to influence their divergent abilities.

For most of the tests there was a satisfactory increase in raw scores from 11 to 15 and the stability of the tests seemed to hold up reasonably well over this time-span, the re-test correlations for non-verbal, verbal and total divergent scores ranging from 0.50 to 0.62. The divergent tests, therefore, in general behaved like measures of fairly stable cognitive abilities.

In an investigation in primary schools, Spaulding (1963), too, found strong negative relations between the expression of creativity in elementary-aged children and teacher behaviour characterized as formal group instruction, using shame as a punishment technique, whilst Sears (1963) found positive correlations between creativity and teachers' use of the technique of rewarding children by personal interest in their ideas rather than by evaluation.

As to what lies at the root of this relationship between classroom climate and divergent ability we can only speculate. Children are provided with a model of self-initiated learning and exploration when learning is to some extent based on individual projects involving personal research in the library. In addition, it is likely that creative efforts are stimulated by the teacher's confidence in the child's ability to think adventurously and in new directions, which, in turn, will determine the child's estimation of himself and of his abilities. As we have noted earlier, a necessary condition of creativeness appears to be a certain self-confidence and, particularly, an absence of anxiety about non-conformist responses. Torrance (1967b) suggests the following lines of action if we want to create a school climate favourable to the development of creative attitudes and abilities:

1. Be respectful of unusual questions
2. Be respectful of the unusual ideas of children
3. Show children that their ideas have value
4. Provide opportunities for self-initiated learning and give credit for it
5. Provide for periods of non-evaluated practice or learning.

It should be noted that it seems to be more difficult to establish a link between the climate of a school and divergent abilities when secondary schools are being investigated, and a colleague and I were unsuccessful in such an attempt (Lytton and Cotton, 1969). This failure may be due to the limitations of the tests, but possibly also to the fact that a certain teaching approach in a secondary school characterizes a department rather than the school, so that it is more difficult to speak of a uniform climate permeating the school as a whole. Similarly, Walker (1967) found that students from high schools rated as 'highly creative', i.e. encouraging originality and invention, did not score more highly on divergent tests than did students from contrasted schools.

Hudson (1968) observed an interesting contrast in the prominence of convergers and divergers in schools with differing social backgrounds. He asked girls in two schools to rate their classmates for conscientiousness, independence and rebelliousness, one school being a grammar school catering mainly for middle- and lower-middle-class girls, the other one being a public school which contained a large proportion of girls from upper-middle-class professional families. The grammar school laid great stress on good manners and deportment, the public school less so. Whether as a result of home background or school climate, girls in the grammar school tended to nominate convergers for both virtues and vices, girls in the public school divergers. Hudson concludes: 'The implication is that either the social background of a school or its climate (or both) helps to determine whether convergers or divergers are in the public eye. A lower-middle class and seemingly more regimented school throws the converger forward and leaves the diverger anonymous; an upper-middle class and slightly more expansive one does the reverse.' Poor lower-middle classes!

Teaching for creativity

Now it is easy to utter resounding and sweeping condemnations of the school system as it exists. No doubt a great deal of present schooling is still a waste of time and effort and even detrimental to the development of children's thinking capacities, with its insistence on the parrotting of unrelated facts, or the mechanical learning of non-understood skills, e.g. the drilling of 'number bonds' when the child has no concept of the constancy of number in the Piagetian sense, and therefore no grasp of the function of the cardinal number system. (It is true that, as the School Mathematics Group at the University of Illinois has found, computational practice may be a necessary step towards understanding conceptual ideas in mathematics. Unfortunately, some schools or teachers do not trouble to ensure that understanding ever comes, even after practice.) Nevertheless, school and teachers vary in their emphasis, as we have shown in some of the studies mentioned, and it would be unrealistic to tar them all with the same brush.

Improving creative abilities is, at least in part, tantamount to improving the effectiveness of thinking and means that we apply rational thought to the process of education itself. In short, efforts to develop creative behaviour adds up simply to what has long been recognized as 'good education'. The principles expounded by Wertheimer in *Productive Thinking* (1961, first published 1945) are not exactly new, yet they have not always been put into practice and represent an improvement on some existing 'rote' methods.

Listing the principles and some methods that derive from them may seem a work of supererogation and like a declaration by the author that he is in favour of motherhood. Moreover, without the many necessary qualifications which cannot find a place here, prescription of 'good' teaching methods must sound like a rag-bag of platitudes. It is therefore with some reluctance that I undertake this task.

The principles and methods that have been outlined in connection with special training procedures in the last chapter clearly lead to a basic distinction that we ought to make in teaching any area of the curriculum, a distinction between memory and understanding. We shall hardly be satisfied with teaching the simple facts and the date of Magna Carta, or the simple skill of manipulating an algebraic equation without wanting the pupil to be able to apply this skill or the analysis of political forces to another situation or to another period of time. In other words, what we desire is transfer of learning. This has been shown to occur only if in our teaching we work for an understanding of the structure of a topic and of the underlying principles of a problem and then stimulate pupils to find applications of these principles in other fields. Not only principles, but also skills, e.g. in problem-solving, can generalize in this way.

This is not to argue against the importance of a knowledge of facts, for it would be as nonsensical to say the scientist or historian can do without facts as it is to say the poet can do without words. Facts are the building blocks of new solutions, as words are building blocks of poems. What is important about facts is that they are of no use if they are a dead weight of unrelated information, but contrariwise, the worker in any field has to rely on his store of information, partly on the periphery of consciousness, and often far removed from the topic he is concerned with, to provide him with hints for possible solutions. Indeed, the richer and more varied his store of information, the more likely is he to come up with fruitful new ideas, provided he can make use of his knowledge in a flexible manner. 'Connect, only connect!'

If we really want our pupils to use their knowledge creatively there are some things that we can do. Do we let them draw analogies from other subject-matter or seek symbolic equivalents of their experiences in other sensory modalities? Do we provide opportunities in some areas of the curriculum for 'discovering' as well as 'remembering' facts? Do we encourage them to play with facts and ideas, not only repeat them? ('Intellectual playfulness' is a characteristic of divergers.) Do we teach them to be sensitive to problems? (Asking questions and allowing pupils to ask questions that lead to divergent responses is something teachers often find difficult.) Do we teach them that a problem has several interpretations and solutions? In tasks where there is a unique convergent answer, do we allow them to travel different roads to arrive at this answer?

Positive answers to these questions, however, do not bear a simple, straight relationship to ideal teaching, for if one considers many of the practices one sees immediately that limitations and qualifications impose themselves. 'Discovery' versus 'presentation' learning, for instance, needs a more detailed analysis; there are various degrees of 'discovery' learning and what the optimum balance between the known and the unknown, between presentation and discovery, is, may vary for different students and different subject-matter and remains an open question.

These principles have been translated into concrete terms and applied to various fields of study in courses that many teachers in Britain will have become familiar with in recent times. It is beyond the scope of this book to go into details, but some examples are: the Nuffield Science courses for secondary, as well as for primary, schools, the School Mathematics Project, sponsored by the Schools Council, the New Maths programme for primary schools and the Humanities Project, also promoted by the Schools Council.

Some experiments have been carried out in an attempt to increase creative behaviour in primary school children, in a general way, apart from the special training programmes in problem-solving (Covington et al., 1969) discussed in the last chapter. The following are some of the more interesting, and partly surprising, conclusions that Torrance (1964) has drawn from a number of studies involving primary school children and their teachers. After an orientation course designed to train teachers in methods of rewarding children's creative behaviour, classroom teachers seemed to want to reward creative thinking, but many of them were unable to do so effectively because of such factors as their own personality characteristics and their perceptions of social expectations. Teachers who participated in in-service training programmes for developing creative thinking did not tend to initiate any more creative activities than their colleagues under control conditions. Unevaluated ('off-the-record') practice tended to produce greater originality, elaboration and sensitivity than evaluated practice in most instances, except at the sixth-grade (eleven-year-old) level. Competition in grades one to six increased fluency, flexibility, and originality in creative-thinking tasks. Practice and 'warm-up' did not completely eliminate the advantage achieved by competition. Individuals tended to achieve along the lines in which they were rewarded. When rewarded for originality, sixth-grade children produced about twice as many original ideas as when they were rewarded for quantity regardless of quality. When one member of a group was definitely superior to the others in creative thinking abilities, he almost always experienced pressures to reduce his productivity or originality and was frequently not given credit for the positive contribution he made to the group's success. (A finding that should give pause to the enthusiasts for the advantages of the group process in enhancing creativity.) When grouping was carried out, homogeneous grouping for tasks requiring creative problem solving reduced the social stress, enabled less creative members to become more productive, and increased the enjoyment of members. (This intriguing conclusion contradicts the prevailing 'progressive' philosophy and some other learning research.) Lastly Torrance concludes that children in grades three to six can be stimulated to do a great deal of writing on their own, if they are given reasons for doing so, e.g. by having a school magazine to write for.

If Torrance found that instructing teachers in methods of rewarding creative behaviour was largely unsuccessful, he did notice differences between teachers in this respect depending on their personality. He gave teachers a 'Motivations Inventory', scored for creativity or other motivation and found that children—in Kindergarten and Grades one to three—taught by teachers who expressed strong creative motivation, improved more than children in classes of teachers who expressed strong critical or control motivation (Torrance, 1965).

The conclusion that we must obviously draw from this is that if we want to stimulate creative change in the school system we must begin, not with methods, but with the persons who make up the institution, and get them to change themselves. Barron (1969) has been engaged in precisely this endeavour and found that involving teachers and administrators as persons was instrumental in securing their attention and commitment. The persons in charge of the programme combined a living-in assessment (similar to the one used with architects etc.) with a loose kind of semi-therapeutic personal relationship with the teachers. The initial 'retreat' was followed up by smaller weekend meetings with interviews concerning the teachers' life histories, philosophy and attitudes—but no training in method. As part of the strategy of engaging the personal interest of the members, the organizers also communicated the results of the personality tests to them at one of the later meetings. The teachers were given various tests of divergent thinking, as well as the Barron-Welsh Art Scale, before and after the course, and significant gains were registered on these measures at the end of the programme.

It will be of interest to quote the personality profiles of one 'No Change' Case and one 'Conspicuous Change' Case, both based on 'blind' interpretation of the personality tests.

'NO CHANGE' CASE

This 45-year-old man is a highly responsible, stable, conventional, slightly rigid individual, perhaps a bit too 'good' for his own good, yet withal an effective model of probity for the young. He appears to be somewhat passive, and he could conceivably have a problem in sexual identity (with fantasies and near-action impulses coming into the picture occasionally). He is so conscientious, however, and also so suppressed, that one would not expect any over pathology. He is likely to be nurturant, perhaps even motherly, in his attitude towards the boys he teaches. The psychic cost to him of the defenses he must maintain is fairly heavy. A chronic mild depression is likely. He can also swing toward paranoia easily, although his expression of it would be muted. He is quite self-critical. In general, he can be described as a deferent, self-abasing, fearful individual, lacking in assertiveness, who gets along by being orderly, obedient, cautious, openly dependent on others, supportive of the status quo, and the enemy of no one.

'CONSPICUOUS CHANGE' CASE

This 47-year-old man is a notably stable and effective individual, yet he is markedly lacking in self-esteem. He is temperate and deliberate in manner, does not like to push himself, and would easily be underrated at first meeting. He is quite astute in his psychological evaluations of others, notably flexible and independent, and unobtrusively efficient. His responsibility and self-control make him someone to rely on over the long haul. He conforms easily, but he clearly values independence and a certain amount of criticism of social norms, and he himself is basically an independent thinker in spite of his manner and general style of representing himself. He has more sympathy for social deviance than one might expect. Why his self-esteem is low is the most important question one can ask about him. This is holding him back. He needs assurance, but exactly what would be reassuring is not clear. He probably knows consciously that he is quite capable. The matter would probably be worth his exploring in depth. (Barron, 1969)

Specialization in arts or science

We now come to a problem that affects the upper end of the secondary school and that is especially acute in England, because here specialization in arts or science takes place at a particularly early age, often at fourteen. Since this choice at fourteen often decides later sixth-form choices which in turn most usually determine the subjects read at University, it has been said with some justification that in England manpower planning is in the hands of fourteen-year-olds. From the individual's point of view, too, such early irrevocable choices close doors and confine future career decisions within narrow limits at an extraordinarily young age. Moreover, intellectually it has the effect of putting blinkers on a young boy and girl and will promote a possibly premature crystallization and narrowing of interests, and with it, conceivably, a certain fixing and establishing of personality lines at a period when these might still be much more fluid. For these reasons many educationists have wished to postpone such decisions to later stages and have advocated a generally broader sixth-form curriculum. This has already had the effect of bringing into sixth forms large groups of students, who, although they are only taking two or three A-level subjects, combine, say, biology with English and history, and can therefore no longer be said to be pure arts or science specialists.

Hudson's (1966) research, however, dealt with pure arts and science specialisms which he related to divergent or convergent thinking abilities. His main conclusion is that arts specialists are mainly divergers in the sense that they do *relatively* better on divergent than on convergent tests, physical scientists are mainly convergers. In his investigation he noted that far more divergers went into subjects like English, history and modern languages, far more convergers into mathematics, physics and chemistry. Classics, in his sample, belonged with physical science, while biology, geography and economics attracted convergers and divergers in roughly equal proportions. A repeat of this experiment (Hudson, 1968, Appendix A) produced very similar results.

Science, while it tends to unique, i.e. convergent, solutions, and depends on an established corpus of facts for its execution, also, of course, must draw on qualities such as imagination and flexibility, if its practitioners are to expand the frontiers of knowledge. However, sixth-form science, until the advent of the new science courses, consisted chiefly in the acquisition of facts and experimental skills. Hudson (1966) saw two dangers in the relationships that he uncovered: '(a) that our Sixth Forms may be attracting boys who are too rigid and inflexible for research; and (b) that scientific education, instead of counteracting boys' natural inflexibility, tends to reinforce and aggravate it'. However, his investigation—carried out on very able boys in grammar and public schools—classified divergers and convergers by the *bias*, not the *level*, of their abilities (see above). It was therefore quite possible for a boy to have a very high divergent score and yet to be classified as a converger, simply because his IQ was relatively even higher. The *level* of divergency exhibited by physical scientists may, indeed, have been quite sufficient for any amount of original research and may even possibly have equalled that of arts specialists. Some of the case studies quoted by Hudson indicate this was in fact the case for some scientists.

Together with some associates (Bevan, 1969, Haddon and Lytton, 1971) I have investigated the question whether arts and science specialists in mixed grammar schools differ significantly in level of divergent ability. While our numbers are smaller than Hudson's, they are sufficient to base conclusions on (108 subjects in the first, 139 in the second, study) and these are that arts and science specialists do *not* differ significantly on divergent tests, though arts specialists have slightly higher scores on verbal divergent tests, as well as somewhat higher IQs. The choice between arts and science was, in fact, largely a function of sex, and not of convergent/divergent ability, boys opting for science, girls for arts. An unexpected discovery in the second study was that the group who had chosen a mixture of arts and science subjects had lower divergent scores (but higher IQs) than those who had made a narrower, but perhaps more committed, choice, in either arts or science. Is high divergent ability related to decisive commitment to a defined band of subjects and perhaps indicative of strength of motivation? One would not like to be definite about this without further confirmation.

It seems, then, that though science specialists may have a bias towards convergent thinking and arts specialists towards divergent thinking, it is too simple an account to think of science sixth formers as pure convergers without a spark of originality who went in for science because of the convergent nature of science teaching, i.e. essentially for the wrong reason. Choice of a career will be determined by many factors and the attitude the school adopts towards various professions and the prestige in which they are held will naturally play an important part in this. It is obvious, too, that unimaginative teachers and dull teaching can deter youngsters from entering certain fields. But also there are myths surrounding the scientist or the man of letters which Hudson (1968) has shown are entertained in broadly identical fashion by adolescents of differing specialisms. The adolescent may well be influenced by them, feeling himself in tune with one or the other of these stereotypes. Material factors, such as economic opportunity and prospects, pressures from school and family, will also play a role, and, above all—as we saw in chapter 3—the young man and woman will be influenced, consciously or otherwise, by his contacts with those around him which helped to shape his basic personality.

6

Retrospect

Why all the stress on 'creativity' at this particular period? It seems to me this groundswell has arisen as a symptom of revolt against the threatening mechanization of man and society, which also shows signs of engulfing the schools. The movement is particularly strong in America, partly because mechanization there has gone farther than in Britain, and partly because the crusade for 'creativity' has somehow got mixed up with a protest against excessive social emphasis in the schools and has become a plea to the American High School to produce independent and intelligent thinkers rather than merely conformist good mixers. (Getzels and Jackson see creativity almost as an antidote to too much 'togetherness'.) The emphasis on creativity also coincides with a need, generally felt in Britain as elsewhere, for the schools to emerge from formalism, traditional routine and drill and the straitjacket of conventional subject divisions. 'Innovation' is the rallying cry of this new movement.

Devotees of education are perhaps particularly prone to fall an easy prey to new watchwords and slogans. A few critical words are therefore not out of place. We must not overemphasize the effect that schools have on children. Quite apart from the biological 'givens' that children bring with them, a multitude of forces in their environment impinge on them, each of which helps them to grow a little and even 'teaches' them without intending to. The school can reinforce or inhibit certain tendencies, but can it turn real convergers into true divergers? In common with Hudson (1966), I think this is doubtful. A distinction between convergent and divergent traits, independent of intelligence, has been shown faintly as early as in the pre-school years and certainly in the primary grades. Divergency is therefore not likely to be entirely under the control of the school.

However, in our critical consideration we should not overlook either the positive evidence which has been marshalled in chapters 4 and 5. Certain attitudes towards self-initiated learning and exploration can, it seems, be fostered successfully, curiosity can be awakened and thinking skills can be made more efficient. Children will gain by any such honest, intelligent effort at good teaching. 'The shrewd guess, the fertile hypothesis, the courageous leap to a tentative conclusion—these are the most valuable coin of the thinker at work, whatever his line of work. Can school children be led to master this gift?' (Bruner, 1960). The answer would seem to be: 'To a certain extent, yes.' On the other hand, there is the danger that under the banner of 'innovation', 'creativity' reigns supreme in the classroom while evaluation flies out of the window. Even teaching by inquiry methods can be inappropriately handled in certain circumstances, can become rigidly stereotyped and meaningless. However, by allowing children to enjoy the creativeness that is in them, by encouraging them to let their fantasies roam as well as to use their critical powers, learning itself can be made more enjoyable and school a happier place.

The purpose of this book has been to give its readers an understanding of the issues that teaching creative children and teaching children to be creative raises for education. It has attempted to clarify how far research has taken us in exploring the relations between convergent and divergent thinking and to show what it can tell us—and what it cannot tell us—about the kind of individual that a creative person is and about the sort of environment that helps him to grow. There is always the danger of a sensible new development becoming a fad. I have therefore eschewed superficial, uncritical enthusiasm, and have tried not to nourish facile illusions. Of course, innovations would never get off the ground if their introduction had to await the outcome of research, and often they have to be started on the basis of a hunch and an ounce of faith. However, in casting a critical eye on the present state of knowledge I hope I have encouraged teachers, on their part, to ally enthusiasm with discrimination in assessing the claims of new ideas and methods.

Appendix

The following pages show the tests that some colleagues and I used in our investigations, and provide illustrations of the productions of eleven-year-olds. The tests have all been derived from the Minnesota Tests of Creative Thinking (Torrance, 1962), except for the Block Printing Test which was devised by Mr F. A. Haddon, Rolle College, Exmouth.

Imaginative Stories

Write the most interesting and exciting story you can about one of the titles suggested below. Try to write so your story can be read but do not worry too much about your writing or spelling. Try to put as many good ideas as you can into your story.

1. The teacher who doesn't talk
2. The hen that crows
3. The dog that won't fight
4. The flying monkey
5. The boy who wants to be a nurse
6. The girl who wants to be an engineer
7. The cat that likes to swim
8. The doctor who became a carpenter
9. The duck that doesn't quack
10. The cow that brays like a donkey.

A sample product, with the original spelling intact
Title: The flying monkey

One day a rather funny thing happened to me I saw a monkey. Now this Monkey was no odanary monkey because this monkey flew. How it flew we don't know beauce it just flew. this monkey was a very brainless monkey it had to have an owner to help it to learn new tricks. It was working at a circus one day when all of a sudden it went mad and flew right through the circis tent! out side was a villain and he thought that if he captured the monkey he could train it to rob banks. So he captured the monkey in a net and after about 6-weeks he had trained it to flew and rob banks or flew after a aircraft and capture it and get the cargo. (it also was able to rob ships.) The villain let the monkey go and it flew after the aircraft just as planned but the monkey thought 'If I could get the aircraft frighten the man who drives it I would be able to fly without useing my own wings.' The monkey got on to the aircraft frightened the pilot and was able to fly without his power. (the pilot flew it for him) While back at the villains hide out, 'where is that monkey?' he cried 'where is it'? in the plane the monkey was having a lovely time he flew and flew with out the use of his wings. After a long time the monkey thought I have had anoth of this so he said to the pilot 'I am going so he jump out of his window and starded to flap his wings but nothing happened he started to fall he fell and fell and fell to his death. After his death the pilot of the plane said 'he must have stayed in the plane to long and his musles were not ready for him to fly agian.' the villain was very sad.

THE END

BLOCK PRINTING TEST
(Devised by Mr F. A. Haddon, Rolle College, Exmouth)

Instructions

Use the block of wood and the ink pad to discover as many different ways of making marks as you can. Put a number by each new mark you have made.

When you have discovered all the marks that you can, you may go on to use these marks in any way you choose. These need not be numbered.

If you want another booklet, ask the person in charge for one.

A sample product

VAGUE SHAPE OF DOTS

Here is a rather vague shape. What could you turn it into? Try to think of something no one else will think of and develop this into a picture. When you have finished, think of a name or title for it and write it at the bottom.

Name or Title .A.. ...Old.....mans....Face......

IDEAS FOR USING AN OLD SHOE BOX

Put each idea on a new line. You need not write sentences as
long as the idea is clear.

1. Make a dolls house
2. keeping things in
3. Pack Preasants in it.
4. ~~Paid~~ keep pencils in it
5. Use it ase a step
6. grow plants in it
7. Make a pin hole camerra whith it
8. Put a hole in it and use it as a watering can
9. make a mask out of it
10. make a bed of staw for a tortiose to sleep in
11. use it as a play letter box
12. keep food in it
13. Use it as a table for dolls
14.
15.
16.
17.
18.

PROBLEMS THAT MIGHT ARISE IN TAKING A BATH

This is a test to see how good you are at thinking out what problems might arise when you are planning to do something.
A. Imagine you are going to have a bath. What are all the awkward things that could happen. Write down as many as you can think of. Put each new idea on a new line. You need not write whole sentences as long as your idea is clear.

1 .. Dads ...... in. the ...... bath ..... room ..... showering.............
2 ... There ..... is ..... no .... soap ..... to. wash.................
3 . I. can ...... not ..... fined ..... my. Pjamas.................
4 .. Mum ...... forgot ...... to .... put ..... the .. heater ... on .....
5 .. The ...... towel .... is ...... to ..... damp. to. dry in ...
6 ... I ..... but .... Persil. in. instead ..... of .... Matey ....
7 ... My .... towel ...... fell ...... in .. my .... bath.............
8 . I ...... lost ...... the .... little ...... bit of. soap ... down. the drain
9 ....
10 ....
11 ....
12 ....
13 ....
14 ....
15 ....
16 ....
17 ....
18 ....

CIRCLES TEST

See how many objects you can make from the circles below by adding lines inside or outside the circle, or both inside and outside. Try to think of as many different things as you can which no one else will think of. Put as many ideas as you can into each one. If your idea is not very clear you may put a title underneath the circle.

Bibliography

Many references are of a technical nature. Books that will be of the most use are in the Further Reading list, preceded here by an asterisk.

ANDERSON, H. H. (ed.) (1959), *Creativity and its Cultivation*, New York: Harper & Row.

*BARRON, F.

BARTLETT, F. C. (1958), *Thinking*, George Allen & Unwin.

BEITTEL, K. R. (1964), 'Creativity in the visual arts in higher education', in C. W. Taylor (ed.), *Widening Horizons in Creativity*, New York, Wiley.

BEREITER, C., and ENGELMANN, S. (1966), *Teaching Disadvantaged Children in the Preschool*, Englewood Cliffs, New Jersey: Prentice-Hall.

BEVAN, F. D. (1969), 'A creativity study in a rural grammar school', unpublished dissertation for the Diploma in Education, University of Exeter.

BRUNER, J. S. (1960), *The Process of Education*, Cambridge, Mass.: Harvard University Press.

—— (1962), 'The conditions of creativity', in Gruber, Terrell and Wertheimer.

BURT, C., and MOORE, R. C. (1912), *Journal of Experimental Pedagogy*, *1*, 251 ff.

*BUTCHER, H. J.

CATTELL, R. B., and DREVDAHL, J. E. A. (1955), 'Comparison of the personality profile (16 PF) of eminent researchers with that of eminent teachers and administrators and of the general population', *British Journal of Psychology*, *46*, 248-61.

COCTEAU, J. (1952), 'The process of inspiration', in Ghiselin.

COLERIDGE, S. T. (1954), *Complete Poems*, London: Macdonald.

CONANT, J. B. (1945), *General Education in a Free Society*, Cambridge, Mass.: Harvard University Press.

COVINGTON, M. V., CRUTCHFIELD, R. S., and DAVIES, L. B. (1969), *The Productive Thinking Program*, Columbus, Ohio: Charles E. Merrill.

CROPLEY, A. J. (1966), 'Creativity and intelligence', *British Journal of Educational Psychology*, 36, 259-66.

*CROPLEY, A. J.

CROSS, H. J. (1966), 'The relation of parental training conditions to conceptual level in adolescent boys', *Journal of Personality*, 34 (3).

CRUTCHFIELD, R. S. (1962), 'Conformity and creative thinking', in Gruber, Terrell, and Wertheimer.

—— (1965), 'Instructing the individual in creative thinking', *New Approaches to Individualising Instruction*, Princeton, New Jersey: Educational Testing Service.

DACEY, J., MADAUS, G., and ALLEN, A. (1969), 'The relationship of creativity and intelligence in Irish adolescents', *British Journal of Educational Psychology*, 39, 261-6.

DEWING, K. (1970), 'The reliability and validity of selected tests of creative thinking in a sample of 7th grade West Australian children', *British Journal of Educational Psychology*, 40, 35-42.

DREVDAHL, J. E. (1964), 'Some developmental and environmental factors in creativity', in C. W. Taylor (ed.), *Widening Horizons in Creativity*, New York: Wiley.

ELLIOTT, J. M. (1964), 'Measuring creative abilities in public relations and in advertising work', in *ibid*.

*FREEMAN, J., BUTCHER, H. J., and CHRISTIE, T.

FREUD, S. (1938), *The Basic Writings of Sigmund Freud*, translated and edited by A. A. Brill, New York: Random House.

—— (1970), 'Creative writers and day-dreaming' (1908), in P. E. Vernon (ed.), *Creativity*, London: Penguin.

*GETZELS, J. W., and JACKSON, P. W.

GHISELIN, B. (1952), *The Creative Process*, New York: Mentor Books, New American Library.

GORDON, W. J. J. (1961), *Synectics: The Development of Creative Capacity*, New York: Harper.

GOUGH, H. G. (1961), 'Techniques for identifying the creative research scientist', *Conference on the Creative Person*, Berkeley: University of California, Institute of Personality Assessment and Research.

*GRUBER, H. E., TERRELL, G., and WERTHEIMER, M.

GUILFORD, J. P. (1950), 'Creativity', *American Psychologist*, 5, 444-54.

—— (1959), 'Three faces of intellect', *American Psychologist*, 14, 469-79.

*GUILFORD, J. P. (1968).

HADAMARD, J. (1952), in Ghiselin.

HADDON, F. A., and LYTTON, H. (1968), 'Teaching approach and the development of divergent thinking abilities in primary schools', *British Journal of Educational Psychology*, 38, 171-80.

—— (1971), 'Teaching approach and divergent thinking abilities—four years on', *ibid.*, 41, 136-47.

HARVEY, O. J. (1966), 'System structure, flexibility and creativity', in O. J. Harvey (ed.), *Experience, Structure and Adaptability*, New York: Springer.

HASAN, P., and BUTCHER, H. J. (1966) 'Creativity and intelligence: a partial replication with Scottish children of Getzels' and Jackson's study', *British Journal of Psychology*, 57, 129-35.

HELSON, R. (1966), 'Personality of women with imaginative and artistic interests: the role of masculinity, originality, and other characteristics in their creativity'. *Journal of Personality*, 34, 1-25.

*HUDSON, L. (1966).

HUDSON, L. (1968), *Frames of Mind. Ability, Perception and Self-Perception in the Arts and Sciences*, London: Methuen.

HUNT, J. MCV. (1961), *Intelligence and Experience*, New York: Ronald Press.

HUTCHINSON, E. D. (1960), *How to Think Creatively*, New York: Abingdon-Cokesbury, 1949, summarized in Stein and Heinze.

JACKSON, P. W., and MESSICK, S. (1968), 'Creativity', in P. London and D. Rosehan (eds.), *Foundations of Abnormal Psychology*, New York: Holt.

JENSEN, A. R. (1969), 'How much can we boost I.Q. and scholastic achievement?', *Harvard Educational Review*, 39, 1-123.

JUNG, C. G. (1933), *Modern Man in Search of a Soul*, New York: Harcourt, Brace and World.

KOESTLER, A. (1959), *The Sleepwalkers*, London, Hutchinson.

*KOESTLER, A. (1964).

KRIS, E. (1952), *Psycho-analytic Exploration in Art*, New York: Schocken.

KUBIE, L. S. (1958), *Neurotic Distortion of the Creative Process*, University of Kansas Press.

LYTTON, H., and COTTON, A. C. (1969), 'Divergent thinking abilities in secondary schools', *British Journal of Educational Psychology*, 39, 188-90.

MACKINNON, D. W. (1962), 'The nature and nurture of creative talent', *American Psychologist*, 17, 484-95.

MACKINNON, D. W., *et al.* (1961), *Proceedings of the Conference on 'The Creative Person'*, University of California Alumni Center, Lake Tahoe, California, Berkeley: University of California Extension.

MALTZMAN, I. (1955), 'Thinking: from a behaviorist point of view', *Psychological Review*, 62, 275-86.

MANN, T. (1967), *Doktor Faustus*, Frankfurt am Main: Fischer Buecherei.

MCHENRY, R. E., and SHOUKSMITH, G. A. (1970), 'Creativity, visual imagination and suggestibility: their relationship in a group of 10-year old children', *British Journal of Educational Psychology*, 40, 154-60.

MENDELSSOHN, G. A., and GRISWOLD, B. B. (1966), 'Assessed creative potential, vocabulary level and sex as predictors of the use of incidental cues in verbal problem solving', *Journal of Personality and Social Psychology*, 4, 423-33.

MILLER, D. R., and SWANSON, G. D. (1958), *The Changing American Parent*, New York: Wiley.

MILNER, MARION (1958), 'Psycho-analysis and art', in J. D. Sutherland, *Psychology and Contemporary Thought*, London: Hogarth Press.

MOONEY, R. L. (1967), 'Creation in the classroom setting', in R. L. Mooney and T. A. Razik (eds.), *Explorations in Creativity*, New York: Harper and Row.

*MOONEY, R. L., and RAZIK, T. A. (eds.).

MOORE, O. K. (1966), 'Autotelic responsive environments and exceptional children', in O. J. Harvey (ed.), *Experience, Structure and Adaptability*, New York: Springer.

NEWELL, A., SHAW, J. C., and SIMON, H. A. (1962), 'The process of creative thinking', in Gruber, Terrell and Wertheimer.

NICHOLS, R. C., and HOLLAND, J. L. (1963), 'Prediction of the first year college performance of high aptitude students', *Psychological Monographs*, 77, 1-29.

OLTON, R. M., and CRUTCHFIELD, R. S. (1969), 'Developing the skills of productive thinking', in P. H. Mussen, J. Langer and M. Covington (eds.), *Trends and Issues in Developmental Psychology*, New York: Holt, Rinehart and Winston.

OSBORN, A. F. (1953), *Applied Imagination*, New York: Scribners.

PARNES, S. J. (1963), 'Education and creativity', *Teachers' College Record*, 64, 331-9.

PINES, M. (1966), *Revolution in Learning*, New York: Harper & Row.

POINCARÉ, H. (1913), 'Mathematical creation', in *The Foundation of Science*, New York: Science Press.

REXROTH, K. (1957), 'The vivisection of a poet', *Nation*, 185, 450-3.

RILKE, R. M. (1939), *Duino Elegies*, translation and introduction by J. B. Leishman and S. Spender, London: Hogarth Press.

ROE, A. (1952), 'A psychologist examines sixty-four eminent scientists', *Scientific American*, 187, 21-5.

—— (1953), 'A psychological study of eminent psychologists and anthropologists and a comparison with biological and physical scientists', *Psychological Monographs*, 67, No. 352.

SCHAEFER, C. E., and ANASTASI, A. (1968), 'A biographical inventory for identifying creativity in adolescent boys', *Journal of Applied Psychology*, 52, 42-8.

SEARS, P. (1963), 'The effect of classroom conditions on the strength of achievement, motive and work output of elementary school children', Stanford University (U.S. Office of Education Co-operative Research Project No. 873) (mimeographed).

SPAULDING, R. (1963), 'Achievement, creativity and self-concept correlates of teacher-pupil transactions in elementary schools', Urbana, Ill.: University of Illinois (U.S. Office of Education Co-operative Research Project No. 1352) (mimeographed).

SPENDER, S. (1946), 'The making of a poem', *Partisan Review*.

STEIN, M. I. (1963a), 'Creativity and culture', *Journal of Psychology*, 36, 311-22.

—— (1963b), 'A transactional approach to creativity', in C. W. Taylor and F. Barron (eds.), *Scientific Creativity: its Recognition and Development*, New York: Wiley.

STEIN, M. I., and HEINZE, S. J. (1960), *Creativity and the Individual*, Chicago: Free Press.

STORR, A. (1968), 'The concept of cure', in C. Rycroft (ed.), *Psychoanalysis Observed*, London: Penguin.

TAYLOR, C. W., and BARRON, F. (eds.) (1963), *Scientific Creativity: its Recognition and Development*, New York: Wiley.

TAYLOR, D. W., BERRY, P. C., and BLOCK, C. H. (1958), 'Does group participation when using brainstorming facilitate or inhibit creative thinking?', *Admin. Sci. Quart.*, 3.

TERMAN, L. M., *et al.* (1926-59), *Genetic Studies of Genius*. 5 vols, Stanford University Press.

THOMPSON, W. R. (1966), 'Early experiential and genetic influences on flexibility', in O. J. Harvey (ed.), *Experience, Structure and Adaptability*, New York: Springer.

THORNE, A. (1967), 'Suggestions for mothering the gifted', in J. C. Gowan, G. D. Demos and E. P. Torrance (eds.), *Creativity: Its Educational Implications*, New York: Wiley.

TORRANCE, E. P. (1962), *Guiding Creative Talent*, Englewood Cliffs, New Jersey: Prentice-Hall.

—— (1963), *Education and the Creative Potential*, University of Minnesota Press.

—— (1964), 'Education and creativity', in C. W. Taylor (ed.), *Creativity: Progress and Potential*, New York: McGraw-Hill.

*TORRANCE, E. P. (1965).

—— (1967a), 'Different predictors, criteria and routes to criteria', in J. C. Gowan, G. D. Demos and E. P. Torrance (eds.), *Creativity: Its Educational Implications*, New York: Wiley.

—— (1967b), 'Give the devil his dues', in *ibid*.

TRILLING, L. (1955), 'Art and neurosis', in *The Liberal Imagination*, London: Secker & Warburg.

VERNON, P. E. (1967a), 'A cross-cultural study of "creativity tests" with 11-year-old boys', *New Research in Education*, *1*, 135-46.

—— (1967b), 'Psychological studies of creativity', *Journal of Child Psychology and Psychiatry*, 8, 153-66.

*VERNON, P. E. (ed.) (1970).

VINACKE, W. E. (1960), *The Psychology of Thinking*, New York: McGraw-Hill, 1952, summarized in Stein and Heinze.

WALKER, W. J. (1967), 'Creativity and high school climate', in J. C. Gowan, G. D. Demos, and E. P. Torrance (eds.), *Creativity: Its Educational Implications*, New York: Wiley.

WALLACH, M. A., and KOGAN, N. (1965), *Modes of Thinking in Young Children: A Study of the Creativity-Intelligence Distinction*, New York: Holt.

WALLACH, M. A., and WING, C. W. (1969), *The Talented Student. A Validation of the Creativity-Intelligence Distinction*, New York: Holt.

WALLAS, G. (1926), *The Art of Thought*, London: Cape.

WATSON, J. (1968), *The Double Helix*, London: Weidenfeld & Nicolson.

WEISBERG, P. S., and SPRINGER, K. J. (1961), 'Environmental factors in creative function', *Archives of General Psychiatry*, 5, 64-74.

WERTHEIMER, M. (1961), *Productive Thinking*, London: Tavistock.

WILD, C. (1965), 'Creativity and adaptive regression', *Journal of Personality and Social Psychology*, 2, 161-9.

YAMAMOTO, K. (1963), 'Relationships between creative thinking abilities of teachers and achievement and adjustment of pupils', *Journal of Experimental Education*, 32, 2-25.

—— (1965), 'Effects of restriction of range and test unreliability on correlation between measures of intelligence and creative thinking', *British Journal of Educational Psychology*, 35, 300-5.

Further reading list

BARRON, F. (1969), *The Creative Person and the Creative Process*, New York: Holt. Provides a readable and connected account of the research into the personality characteristics of creative architects and others, carried out at the University of California at Berkeley.

BUTCHER, H. J. (1968), *Human Intelligence: its Nature and Assessment*, London: Methuen. A highly competent, modern treatment of the topic of intelligence. Contains a good section on research into creativity and its relation to intelligence.

CROPLEY, A. J. (1967), *Creativity*, London: Longmans. A short, sound introduction to the topic. Has a chapter on 'The creative child and his teachers'.

FREEMAN, J., BUTCHER, H. J., and CHRISTIE, T. (1968), *Creativity. A Selective Review of Research*, London: Society for Research into Higher Education. Is exactly what its title indicates: a reliable guide to the research in the subject, with long, even though still selective, bibliographies.

GETZELS, J. W., and JACKSON, P. W. (1962), *Creativity and Intelligence*, New York: Wiley. An account of the authors' study of 'high creatives' and 'high IQ' adolescents together with their views on the importance of creativity in the educational setting. Should be read with a critical eye and in conjunction with the review of the book by Burt in the *British Journal of Educational Psychology*, 1962, 32, 292-8.

GRUBER, H. E., TERRELL, G., and WERTHEIMER, M. (eds.) (1962), *Contemporary Approaches to Creative Thinking*,

New York: Atherton Press. A collection of excellent papers on the broader aspects of creativity, by distinguished contributors who write highly polished prose. Read particularly the papers by Bruner, by Crutchfield and by Newell, Shaw and Simon, listed in the bibliography.

GUILFORD, J. P. (1968), *Intelligence, Creativity and their Educational Implications*, San Diego: Knapp. A collection of lectures and papers giving the views of this famous pioneer on the relations of intelligence and creativity to each other and to educational problems.

HUDSON, L. (1966), *Contrary Imaginations*, London: Methuen. (Also available in Penguin.) A bright book that gives an honest and entertaining account of the author's own investigation together with many interesting, though highly speculative, ideas.

KOESTLER, A. (1964), *The Act of Creation*, London: Hutchinson. A long, rambling book that provides a stimulating literary (not scientific) theory of the act of creation. Also contains many interesting, but waspish disquisitions on the present state of psychology based on somewhat one-sided reading of the psychological literature of the 40s and 50s.

MOONEY, R. L., and RAZIK, T. A. (eds.) (1967), *Explorations in Creativity*, New York: Harper & Row. A collection of some more, some less, interesting papers. Contains sections on the nature and nurture of creativity, on the measurement of creativity and on instructing in creative thinking.

TAYLOR, C. W. (ed.) (1964), *Creativity: Progress and Potential*, New York: McGraw-Hill. Contains some longer chapters on the predictors of creative performance, environment and training for creativity, criteria of creativity and, especially, on education and creativity (the last by Torrance).

TORRANCE, E. P. (1965), *Rewarding Creative Behavior*, Englewood Cliffs: Prentice-Hall. Provides an account of the author's courses for teachers on rewarding creative thinking, courses which were only partially successful. Has many suggestions on how to treat creative talent at school, written with missionary zeal.

VERNON, P. E. (ed.) (1970), *Creativity*, London: Penguin. A very wide-ranging book of readings, with sections on pioneer empirical studies, introspective materials, theoretical contributions, psychometric approaches, personality studies and on stimulating creativity. The papers range in date from 1789 (Mozart) to 1968.